hd

MYSTICAL MAGIC

MYSTICAL MAGIC

IVOR BADDIEL ★ JONNY ZUCKER

14289350

Hippo

For Ruby and Jake

Thanks to Lisa Edwards, Jill Sawyer
and Peter Lamont

Scholastic Children's Books,
Euston House, 24 Eversholt Street,
London NW1 1DB, UK

A division of Scholastic Ltd
London ~ New York ~ Toronto ~ Sydney ~ Auckland
Mexico City ~ New Delhi ~ Hong Kong

Published in the UK by Scholastic Ltd, 2003

10 digit ISBN 0 439 98117 4
13 digit ISBN 978 0439 981170

All rights reserved
Typeset by Falcon Oast Graphic Art Ltd.
Printed in the UK by CPI Bookmarque, Croydon, CR0 4TD

10

CONTENTS

INTRODUCTION

If you've ever seen a magician disappear into thin air, saw someone in half or even survive for days on end inside a block of freezing-cold ice, we'll bet you were mystified, dumbfounded and bamboozled. We'll also bet that you want to know how magicians do all of these astonishing feats, don't you?

Well, this book will reveal *some* of the tricks of the trade, but not all of them. Magicians are a very secretive bunch and, if we told you too much, they might send us floating to the Moon and never bring us back. So, for some, you'll just have to use your own brainpower to work out how they're done.

What you *will* find out in *Mystical Magic* is how to become a great entertainer and performer of illusions. Because that's what the magic in this book is all about. The magicians you'll be reading about don't have any special, weird powers. They are just ordinary human beings who, because they've done loads and loads of practice, can make it *look* like they're doing amazing things and be very entertaining and mystical at the same time. And if they can do it – so can you.

So, to guide you through a selection of terrific tricks that will amaze and baffle your friends, will you please welcome to the book, the one, the only, the Great Miraculo, and his bumbling assistant, Clumsini.

> Thank you, thank you, thank you. You are too kind. But before I can show you anything at all, I must ask you to do one little thing for me. You must sign the Magician's Charter. Clumsini — if you please...

MAGICIAN'S CHARTER

I................(YOUR NAME) PROMISE NEVER TO TELL ANYONE HOW TO DO ANY OF THE TRICKS I LEARN EVEN IF THEY OFFER ME LOADS OF SWEETS, SWEAR TO DO MY HOMEWORK FOR ME FOR EVER, GIVE ME THEIR POCKET MONEY EVERY WEEK AND PROMISE TO SEND ME ALL THE MONEY THEY EARN FROM THEIR JOB WHEN THEY'RE GROWN UP.

CLAP! CLAP!

CLAP! CLAP!

All done? Good. Now we've got that over with, you can read on and find out:

- whose act included swallowing a gladiator on horseback
- how magicians make objects such as elephants, aeroplanes and even buildings disappear
- why some magicians prefer reading muscles to minds
- how to put on a prize performance of your own.

First off, though, let's find out how some cups made mugs out of ancient audiences...

ANCIENT ANTICS

Magicians first performed for the Pharaohs of ancient Egypt some 4,500 years ago. (There may have been magicians before this but there is no record of them.) We know this because their performances were recorded on the Westcar Papyrus[1], an ancient Egyptian document. In particular, the papyrus tells the story of a chap called Dedi. Apparently, he was 110 years old (quite a magic feat in itself) and could make an animal whose head had been chopped off come back to life. The papyrus says that he did this first with a goose and then with a bull. In each case, he uttered a magic spell, the heads mysteriously reattached themselves and the animal came back to life...

[1] If you want to check out the Westcar Papyrus for yourself, it is on display at the State Museum in Berlin, Germany.

The thing is, no one knows exactly how Dedi did his trick, or if he really did it at all. You see, the story could be a load of bull. The Westcar Papyrus was written 1,000 years after the events it describes, which means that for all that time the story was passed on by word of mouth. It's likely that Dedi performed a slightly less exciting trick, which was then exaggerated over time – a case of Egyptian Chinese whispers. Perhaps whoever wrote the papyrus also wanted the trick to seem more impressive.

How did they do that?
Dedi's head trick.
Geese tuck their heads under their wings to go to sleep and it is possible to train them to do this when you give a special command. Dedi could have pretended to cut the goose's head off, while giving it the command to tuck its head in.

At the same time, he may have produced a very realistic-looking false head, complete with fake blood, to show the audience. Later, he could have pretended to "fix" the head back on, while giving the command for the goose to stick its head out again and secretly getting rid of the fake head.

At around the same time as Dedi, other people were using magic tricks to make themselves appear impressive. Priests and religious leaders in Egypt claimed to have great powers. They made statues of gods "speak" and temple doors suddenly fly open claiming that it was the gods who made these things happen. Of course it wasn't, but an awful lot of people believed them.

After Dedi, stories of magicians with incredible "powers" were told all over the ancient world:

1. In the 1st century AD in Turkey, a magician called Apollonius supposedly made the wedding feast of a nobleman called Menipus vanish – and he also made all the guests disappear as well.

GREAT! NOW WHAT DO I DO WITH ALL THESE SAUSAGE ROLLS?

2. Around the same time, a performer called Iamblichus in the Middle East walked through the air – and changed the colour of his clothes as he did so.

THAT COLOUR REALLY ISN'T HIM...

3. In the AD 800s, an illusionist called Zedekiah made a garden, complete with flowers and trees, appear from nowhere. He also cut a man in half and put him back together. And as if that wasn't enough, he also swallowed a gladiator on horseback, a hay cart, the driver of the cart and all the horses pulling it. Now that's impressive.

It's possible that these ancient tricksters used techniques that were lost over time, and that these skills are still waiting to be rediscovered by today's magicians. But we *do* know how one particular ancient trick was done because it is still being performed today. It's a trick that began some 6,000 years ago and it took the ancient world by storm…

Suddenly, as if by magic, everyone was doing the Cups and Balls trick. OK, maybe not *everyone* in the ancient world was doing it but the trick was certainly being performed in a lot of places at around the same time.

The earliest-known Cups and Balls performance was pictured on the wall of an Egyptian burial chamber in Beni Hassan. Experts reckon that it was painted over 4,000 years ago.

But the trick remained popular for thousands of years – Roman statesman Seneca wrote about it in the first century AD and so did Greek writer Alciphron in the sixth century. Most magic historians think of Cups and Balls as the oldest, and best-known, trick in the book.

Goodness gracious, great balls (and cups)

The basic idea of the trick involves taking three cups and three balls, putting the balls under the cups, moving the cups around and asking people to guess where the balls are. Of course, unless the magician is really bad, the balls are not where the people think they are. Sometimes all three balls have moved to one cup, sometimes two balls are in one cup, one ball is in another cup and one cup is empty. Sometimes all three balls have disappeared and turn up in the magician's pocket!

You're probably itching to find out how the basic trick is done. Well, ladies and gentlemen, to put you out of your misery, to amaze, astound and astonish you, here's the Great Miraculo...

So, you want to know how to do the Cups and Balls trick, eh? Well, before you start, you need three cups and four, yes, four balls. The balls can be pieces of tissue paper scrunched up if you like. Clumsini, cups if you please!

First, secretly push one of the balls firmly into one cup and then stack all the cups together, making sure that the cup with the ball hidden inside is in the middle of the stack.

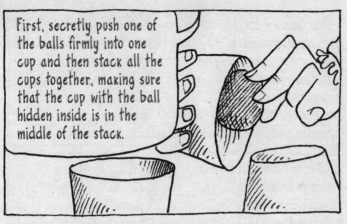

Now you're ready to perform the trick.

With three balls in front of you, quickly and smoothly place the cups down on the table. Make sure that you turn the mouth of the cup with the ball hidden in it slightly towards you as you put it down, so that no one sees the ball.

Now, pick up one of the balls and place it on top of the middle cup, the one with the ball hidden under it.

Take the other two cups and stack them on top of the middle cup.

Say the magic word, Abracahocuspresto, and lift up the stack of cups. Amazingly, the ball appears to have fallen through and on to the table. It may be the oldest trick in the book, but it still dazzles audiences every time.

This version of the trick is one of the simplest. To perform much more complicated versions, where a ball ends up in your mouth or maybe behind your ear, you'll need to know about something called *sleight of hand*. It's a very important magic technique, in fact it's probably how Dedi got rid of that fake goose head, so you might as well learn about it right now...

Tricks of the trade - sleight of hand

This means using your hands to make an audience think that you are doing one thing when really you are doing something else. A classic example of sleight of hand is known as the French Drop. This involves the magician appearing to pass an object from one hand to the other, when in fact the object is secretly dropped into the "passing" hand and remains there. For this example, we've used a marble.

THE MARBLE IS HELD BETWEEN THE THUMB AND FINGER OF ONE OF YOUR HANDS.

THE THUMB OF THE OTHER HAND (HAND 2) THEN PASSES BENEATH THE MARBLE WITH THE OTHER FOUR FINGERS PASSING ON TOP OF IT.

THE THUMB AND THE FINGERS OF HAND 2 CLOSE AROUND THE MARBLE AS IF TO CLASP IT. THE MARBLE IS THEN DROPPED INTO THE PALM OF HAND 1.

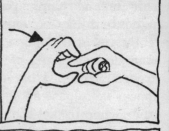

HAND 2 MOVES AWAY WITH FIST CLENCHED TO CREATE THE ILLUSION THAT THE MARBLE IS INSIDE IT.

HAND 2 IS OPENED TO REVEAL THAT THE MARBLE HAS 'DISAPPEARED'. IN FACT, THE MARBLE IS NOW IN HAND 1.

MARBLE

The French Drop is a basic sleight-of-hand technique. Other techniques can involve very speedy movements or clever bending or turning of the hands. It's a skill that's required for many of the tricks in this book – from card stunts to vanishing coins.

The Cups and Balls became so associated with magic that, in many places, the word for magician actually came from the trick:

- The ancient Roman word for magician was *acetabularius*, which came from the Latin word for wine cup or goblet.
- In ancient Greece they used the word *psephopaikteo*, which came from the Greek word for pebbles and their movement under cups.
- In France, magicians were once called *escamouteurs*, which came from the French word for the balls used in the trick.

In the next chapter, you'll discover that whatever they were called, magicians went on to become the most popular *and* most unpopular people around – all at the same time...

MAGIC ON THE MOVE

Up until the 1300s, people in Europe weren't too bothered about magic. But then the Renaissance started in Italy, which meant that European people became very interested in new ideas and new ways of thinking. They wanted to see things that they had never seen before – and magic was one of them. Over the next 200 years, magicians started performing all over Europe and became very popular. They would arrive in a village, set themselves up in a little booth or tent and then gather a crowd around them to watch their performances.

For your amazement
During the Renaissance, magicians mainly performed tricks with balls and coins, and were often referred to as jugglers.

Sounds all very nice and lovely, doesn't it? Well, unfortunately, it wasn't. You see, back then, kings, queens and church leaders were very powerful. They really didn't like anyone who seemed to have weird and wonderful powers that threatened their own. Magicians were often accused of being witches, arrested, put on trial and then executed by hanging, burning or drowning. And, once they were accused, it was very difficult for them to explain that they weren't guilty. Anything they said or did could be twisted around to make it seem like they were admitting to being a witch...

Parchment number 4.1.

To be completed by those possessing magical powers.
Are you a witch?

1. Can you perform magic?

Yes, but that's because I'm a magician.

Almost certainly a witch

2. If you have answered yes to **question 1.** where do you get your magic powers from?

I taught myself to do the tricks because, as I said, I'm a magician. I entertain people with magic. That's how I make a living.

Very witch like

3. Can you chop the head off a goose and then make it come back to life again?

No, but I know of someone who could.

Has witches for friends 99% certain he's a witch ..

4. Are you a witch?

No.

Only a witch would lie about being a witch!

5. Are you not a witch?

Yes, er, hang on, no. No wait, I mean yes.

That's it, he doesn't know if he's not sure that he's not a witch. He's definitely a witch!

Those magicians who were brave enough to try and perform were very often halfway through a trick when someone accused them of using witchcraft. They would then disappear – not magically, you understand, just very, very quickly – and move on to the next village to see how long they'd last there.

ALL RIGHT! ALL RIGHT! I WAS GETTING FED UP WITH THIS PLACE ANYWAY!

For your amazement
In the 1500s magician Triscalinus made the rings from French king Charles IX's fingers come off and float through space – unfortunately the audience then set upon the magician and made him admit to having "demonic" assistance. Sounds like someone pointed the finger at him.

OK, "RING" HIS NECK!

A GREAT DISCOVERIE

But, towards the end of the 1500s, a judge by the name of Reginald Scot, who used to try magicians accused of being witches, became very interested in the amazing acts they performed. So much so that Reg enlisted the help of an entertainer of the day called Cautares, and, with the knowledge he gained, wrote a book called, *The Discoverie of Witchcraft*. (No, it's not that he couldn't spell very well. That's how they spelt it in the 1500s.)

The book was published in 1584 and one chapter, *The Art of Juggling Discovered*, dealt with the magic tricks of the time. It was the first book to explain how magic tricks were done and a lot of the principles it describes are still in use today. There were three sections explaining loads of tricks. Here are a few of them:

1. To consume (or rather to conueie) one or manie balles into nothing.

In other words, to make a ball disappear. According to the book, you take one or more balls in your left hand and appear to put them in your right hand while using "charming words". Actually, what you do is let the balls secretly drop into your lap.

When you open your left hand, people watching will say that the ball or balls are definitely in your right

25

hand and will be greatly shocked when you open your right hand and see that it's empty.

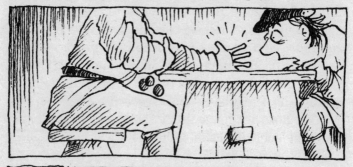

3. To cut half your nose asunder, and to heale it againe presentlie without anie salve.

This trick involves chopping off half your nose, only for it to reappear in perfect shape later. To do it you need a special knife with a round gap in the middle that makes it look like you've cut your nose in half when you use it. (See picture below.) To make the illusion even more believable you have to have another ordinary knife which you secretly swap with the trick knife and then show to people together with plenty of fake blood. (Well it could be real blood, a chicken's or a pig's, just as long as it's not yours.)

The first thing you need to know is that groats and testors were coins, so the trick is one where a coin jumps out of a pot and runs along a table. It seems miraculous until you find out that it's all done by making a tiny hole in the coin and threading a long black hair from a woman's head through it. (The book says it should be a hair from a woman's head, but it could just as easily be from a man's head if his hair was long enough.)

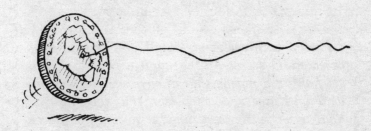

Most importantly, Scot ended the chapter by saying that magic was just a bit of fun really. Harmless entertainment, and most certainly not witchcraft.

For your amazement

At the court of Henry VIII, a magician called Brandon drew a picture of a pigeon on the floor and then struck the centre of the picture with a dagger, at which point a real pigeon sitting on a wall dropped dead. Unfortunately for Brandon, the king reckoned that if he could do that to a bird, he might also be able to do it to the King and so Brandon was told never to do the trick again, if he valued his life! No doubt he was looking daggers at the king when Henry VIII told him.

Pretty impressive trick? Well, Scot's book revealed the secret. All the magician had to do was get hold of a pigeon that always sat on the same wall and give it some poison that took half an hour to work. He then timed it so that the pigeon dropped down dead at the moment he struck the picture with the dagger. Simple, huh? But using the right words and getting the timing spot on made it very, very effective.

Flaming nuisance

Now, you might have thought that the publication of Scot's book was good news for magicians, as people could see that they were simply using illusion for entertainment. Well, unfortunately, James I became king of England in 1603. He really wasn't very keen on witchcraft and decided that something had to be done about it. So what did he do? (There's a clue in the heading by the way.) Did he:

a) Chop the hands off anyone caught reading Scot's book?

b) Throw Reginald Scot in a dungeon and feed him beetles for the rest of his life?

c) Order all copies of the book to be collected and burned?

d) Buy the film rights to the book in the hope that someone might invent moving pictures during his reign?

Unfortunately, the answer is **c)**. But don't worry, there is...

Some good news

EARLIER TODAY, HIS MAJESTY THE KING ORDERED ALL COPIES OF THAT TERRIBLE, TERRIBLE BOOK, **THE DISCOVERIE OF WITCHCRAFT,** TO BE BURNED.

THE ORDER STATES THAT ANYONE IN POSSESSION OF THIS EVIL TOME MUST HAND IT IN TO THE AUTHORITIES WHO WILL BEGIN THE BURNING PROCESS IMMEDIATELY.

WE NOW GO OVER TO OUR REPORTER, PERCY DE GRUYERE, WHO'S BY A BIG BONFIRE...

THANK YOU, CUTHBERT. EARLIER TODAY, AS THE KING'S DECREE BECAME KNOWN, THE AUTHORITIES BEGAN ROUNDING UP THE BOOKS AND IN ACCORDANCE WITH HIS MAJESTY'S WISHES, SETTING THEM ALIGHT...

HOWEVER, I CAN TELL YOU, CUTHBERT, THAT NOT ALL COPIES OF THE BOOK HAVE BEEN BURNED. SOME PEOPLE, IN DEFIANCE OF THE KING'S WISHES, ARE HIDING THE BOOK IN THE HOPE THAT IT MIGHT BE SAVED...

FRANKLY, I WOULDN'T LIKE TO BE ONE OF THOSE PEOPLE AND, JUST IN CASE HIS MAJESTY THINKS I AM, I'D LIKE TO SAY THAT I'M NOT. THIS IS PERCY DE GRUYERE FOR RENAISSANCE TELEVISION, BY A BIG BONFIRE.

THANK YOU, PERCY. OTHER NEWS NOW. IN ITALY, SOME LUNATIC CALLED GALILEO IS CLAIMING THAT THE WORLD IS ROUND...

Yes, thankfully some copies of the book did survive and they're still around today. But if you're thinking of popping into your local bookshop to buy one of them, forget it. Original copies of the book are highly sought after and would cost you several thousand pounds. (You can get modern versions that are much cheaper though.) As for Reginald Scot, not much more is known about him; but it's quite likely that, like a lot of his books, he was fired.

Fawkes he's a jolly good fellow
Now, you've all probably heard of *Guy* Fawkes, but I doubt many of you will have heard of *Isaac* Fawkes. As far as we know they weren't related and Isaac never tried to blow anything up, but he did explode on to the world of magic in the early 1700s, making

quite a big bang. Isaac Fawkes was the first magician to make magic respectable. He also moved from town to town, not because he was chased, but because he was in huge demand. He performed in booths at country fairs, in private homes and in theatres all over England and not one person accused him of being a witch. Or, if you like, no one had the knives out for Fawkes.

Isaac Fawkes worked very hard during his life, often performing six shows a day. A ticket to one of his shows cost one shilling (5p) and he made an awful of lot of money. In fact, when he died in 1731, he had £50,000, which was a fortune in those days. He became the most famous magician of his time and his tricks always went down well, even though his audiences watched him very closely. In fact, they watched Fawkes like hawks.

This is how his most famous illusion, the Egg Bag trick, was described in an advert of the time:

He takes an empty bag, lays it on the table and turns it several times inside out. Then he commands 100 eggs out of it and several showers of Gold and Silver. Then, the bag begins to swell and several sorts of wild fowl run out of it upon the table.

Today's magicians still use something called an egg bag, which is a very simple cloth bag with a hidden pocket in it. Nowadays, there are different types of egg bags and the top magicians have them specially made to fit the size of their hands.

It's very likely that Fawkes used something like this for his Egg Bag trick. He might have shown the audience the empty bag and then, using sleight of hand and something called *misdirection*, produced the eggs out of it.

Tricks of the trade- misdirection

This is a very important magic technique that you're going to be coming across a lot in this book. Magicians use it to take their audience's attention away from what they're really doing. There are a number of different ways it can be done.

1. Space misdirection This means getting your audience to look at a certain place, so that you can do something secretly in another place. You can do this by:

● using your eyes – if you look at your left hand, so will the audience, which means that you can do something secretly with your right hand;

DO YOU THINK ANYONE WILL NOTICE?

- using your fingers – if you point at something, the audience will look at it;
- making a noise – the audience will look in the direction that the noise comes from, especially if it's a sudden noise;

- using your assistant – if you decide to have an assistant in your act, they can help take the audience's attention away while you're doing something secret.

2. Time misdirection This means making your audience think that something is about to happen, when in fact it really happened some time ago. For example, if the audience thinks you are about to make a coin appear in your hand when you say a magic word, they'll be watching your hand very closely when you do actually say the magic word. What they don't know is that you may have secretly put the coin in your hand some time before.

There are other ways you can misdirect your audience, but we'll come to these later.

After Fawkes, magic performances grew bigger and more spectacular. It really was a magic time for magic. But who'd have thought that animal magicians would be the ones to take centre stage...

ASTOUNDING ANIMALS

Throughout history, magicians have used animals in their acts – remember Dedi and his geese and Brandon's pigeons? Today, Siegfried and Roy's act is littered with every kind of animal you could imagine. But did you know that, back in the seventeenth century, the most famous creature in magic history was performing tricks himself?

The mane attraction

Morocco was a beautiful white horse belonging to an English entertainer called Banks in the 1600s. He "talked" by stomping his hoof in answer to questions and his most famous tricks were counting the number of spots on a pair of dice, telling someone how much loose change they had in their pocket and announcing the age of a member of the audience. (It's possible that Banks used a secret command to stop Morocco's hoof at the right number.) Morocco could also dance to music, tell fortunes and do card tricks. In fact he was so clever that if he were alive today, he'd definitely be very, very rich.

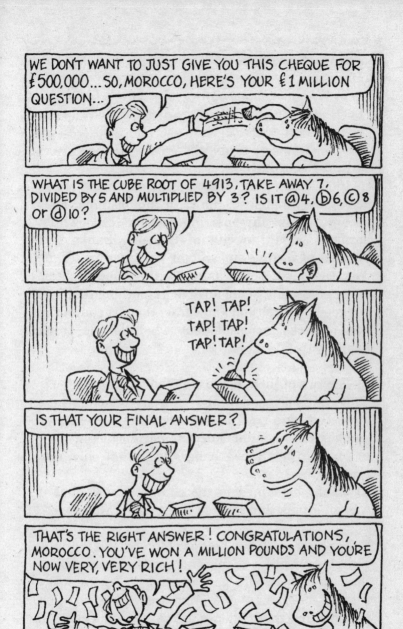

For your amazement
Morocco was so famous that he was even referred to in William Shakespeare's play, Love's Labour's Lost, *and in Sir Walter Raleigh's book,* The History of the World.

Taken for a ride

In 1608, Banks and Morocco saddled up and sailed across the English Channel to tour Europe. They became very famous in France, but whilst performing in the city of Orleans, Banks was accused of owning an animal that was in league with the devil. This was really the same thing as being accused of being a witch, something that was not good news, as you know from the last chapter. It was a tricky situation, but what do you think happened?

a) The two of them made a gallop for it.
b) They went before the church council, where Morocco took a crucifix from someone in the crowd and went down on his knees to beg for mercy.
c) Morocco let Banks hang and set off on a solo career.
d) Banks explained to the church council that it was all a trick and showed them how it was done.

The answer is **b)** and, because Morocco did that, the church council let them both go, as they reckoned that no devil would go near a cross. So, a lucky escape for Banks and Morocco... But it's just possible that they galloped out of the frying pan and into the fire. Some people say that after Orleans they went on to Rome, where they were again charged with being in league with the devil, this time by the Pope himself, and were burned alive. The truth is that no one really knows what became of them, but maybe they got away from Rome and returned home with "neigh" trouble at all.

HOW ARE YOU ENJOYING YOUR TRIP?

HE SAYS, GREAT, SIR.

Rabbit bit

Morocco the horse might be the most famous animal in magic history, but what's the first creature that comes into your head when you think about animals and magic?

Exactly. And what is happening to the rabbit?

Double exactly. But it's something of a mystery. Nobody knows:

a) where the trick came from and who first performed it;

b) why it has become the most famous trick in magic, because it's actually quite difficult to do.

We *do* know (because there are posters showing him doing it) that a magician called John Henry Anderson was performing the trick in the mid-1800s. But Anderson was well known for copying other magicians, so it is possible that he wasn't actually the first person to perform the trick. However it started, though, this is how it was probably done:

How did they do that?
The pull-the-rabbit-out-of-the-hat-trick

1. The magician has a table onstage which has a small hidden hook attached to the back of it. At the start of the trick, the rabbit is hidden in a small bag, which is hung on the hook. (You can't see the bag because of the tablecloth.)

2. The magician shows the audience the empty hat. Then (and here's the difficult bit) he has to scoop the rabbit into the hat in one very quick movement without the audience seeing him do it. This is done using misdirection.

3. With the rabbit safely in the hat, the magician can produce it to the amazement of everyone.

It's important to pick the rabbit up by the scruff of the neck when you are performing this trick. When the trick was first performed magicians picked the rabbits up by their ears, something that is very painful for the animals and causes them to kick their legs around wildly. Unfortunately, in those days magicians liked this because it added excitement and drama to their acts.

A beastly law

Magicians have to follow strict guidelines when they're working with animals. The Performing Animals (Regulation) Act of 1925 says that magicians must register with their local authority if they intend to use animals in their act and they must say how they are going to use the animals. So if you're thinking of using your pet hamster in your act, be warned.

42

It's a dog's life

By the early 1900s, animals were regularly being used in magic acts. One of the most famous was Beauty, a mongrel dog given to the German magician Lafayette by legendary escapologist Harry Houdini. (More about him in on page 132.)

Lafayette was a spectacular entertainer who used a number of animals in his incredible illusions, including Beauty. In one particular illusion – called Dr Kremser Vivisectionist – Lafayette appeared to turn Beauty into a monster, which then attacked Lafayette and seemed to chop his head off.

Incredibly, moments later, Lafayette's head was back in place and Beauty had been transformed once more into a normal dog. The secret of this trick remains a mystery. And audiences loved it, even though they thought that Lafayette was barking mad.

Lafayette and Beauty's lifestyle was as extravagant as their act. The two of them were inseparable – Beauty really was that man's best friend. Here are some of the canine capers they got up to:

Unfortunately, the story of Beauty and Lafayette does not have a happy ending. On 4 May 1911, Beauty died. Lafayette was, of course, devastated and said:

I have lost my dearest friend. Beauty was my mascot, and I feel, I know that I shall not be much longer in this world. Our lives were irrevocably bound together.

WHEN THEY TRAVELLED BY TRAIN, BEAUTY HAD HER OWN COMPARTMENT.

BEAUTY HAD A SILVER AND LEATHER COLLAR ON WHICH WAS ENGRAVED THE NAME OF ALL THE REALLY POSH HOTELS SHE'D STAYED IN.

Spookily his prediction came true. Five days later, an oriental lantern burst into flames onstage just as Lafayette was taking his bow after a performance. The fire grew rapidly, until it was raging uncontrollably. In total, nine people died that night, as well as a lion and a horse. Lafayette's almost unrecognizable body was discovered in the basement of the theatre. He was buried with the embalmed body of Beauty in a vault in Piershill Cemetery in Edinburgh (it's still there today), no doubt happy to be back with the dog he loved so much.

Animals in the 21st century

Nowadays, magicians use just about any animal you can think of in their acts, but some magicians, like American Lance Burton, are famous for one animal in particular. Lance has been astounding audiences since 1980 with his spectacular show, the centrepiece of which is his dove production, where he makes countless doves appear and disappear in stunning displays.

I KNEW I SHOULDN'T HAVE FED THEM BEFORE THE ACT!

Producing a bird onstage isn't really much more difficult than producing a ball, scarf or any other object, but the end product – a live animal opening its wings and taking to the sky – is much more spectacular.

How did they do that?
Producing birds

The main problem, obviously, with making birds appear onstage, is keeping the bird still. Birds naturally stay still in the dark, so this helps, but magicians may also use a special harness. Usually, this is a cloth tube with a loop of wire coming out from one end. The bird is put into the tube with its head sticking out of one end and its tail sticking out of the other. A Velcro fastening at each end of the tube keeps the bird still.

1. Before going onstage, the magician hides the bird in a pocket.

2. During the performance, he secretly slips a finger into the wire loop, lifts out the harnessed bird and puts it in the handkerchief, or whatever he's going to produce it from. (The material of the tube must be the same colour as the material of the handkerchief.) This movement often happens with a flourish.

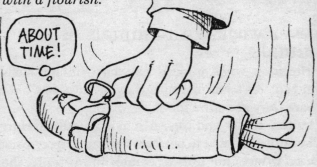

ABOUT TIME!

3. *The magician shows the audience the handkerchief, then whips it down and up again seemingly in one movement, releasing the bird from the handkerchief on the upward movement.*

4. *The magician has really slipped a finger into the loop on the downward motion and ripped open the tube to release the bird on the upward movement. (He may make a noise to cover the sound of the Velcro ripping.) The skill is in making this part of the trick look very smooth.*

Never work with animals or animals

Performing with animals can have its problems, and that isn't just because they're not fussy about where they go to the toilet.

In the 1960s and 70s, a magician called Harry Blackstone Jr used to perform a disappearing camel trick, where he put a camel in a tent, then dismantled the tent to reveal that the camel had vanished. However, on one occasion the animal stuck its head out from behind a false backdrop, ruining the illusion – and giving Harry the hump, no doubt.

The first magician to use chimpanzees in his act was Owen Clark who performed a trick in which a chimp escaped from a box. Unfortunately, he had to stop performing the trick during one performance, as Betty the chimp refused to come out, forcing her trainer to rush onstage and coax her out.

I DON'T CARE IF HOUDINI DOES WANT ME, TELL HIM I'M NOT DOING IT FOR LESS THAN 500 BANANAS!

German magicians Siegfried and Roy have practically an entire zoo onstage with them when they perform. Their show has been flabbergasting folk in Las Vegas, America for 30 years now. It's a beastly performance with elephants, lions, tigers, crocodiles, leopards, panthers, eagles, flamingos and even a fire-breathing metal monster. They make the animals appear, disappear and even shrink. Of course, all their animals are specially trained so that they stay calm onstage and aren't frightened by the bright lights, the noises and all the people looking at them (which is probably the most scary thing). However, theirs is still a highly dangerous act...

During one performance, a lion bit Siegfried on the hand and arm. His arm was sewn up and bandaged but the two magicians had another performance to do that night and, as everyone knows, the show must go on. In the middle of that second performance, Siegfried's stitches burst and blood poured out of his arm. Fortunately, the costume and bandage soaked up most of the blood and he was able to finish the performance, but after the show Roy described his arm as looking like "a clump of raw bloody meat". Uuuurgh!

If we've put you off working with real animals for life, here's the Great Miraculo to show you an animal-related trick that will leave your friends wondering if you really are human…

Ah, hello, hello. I'm glad that you're still with us. Now, for this trick you'll need a pad of paper, a pen, an envelope and some sort of container to put pieces of paper in — a box, a hat, a basket, any such thing will do. Clumsini, a container, please!

Now ask your audience to shout out the names of animals. Any animals they like, from an iguana to a rhinoceros.

As the members of the audience shout out each name, you appear to be writing them all down on separate pieces of paper. But, what you're really doing is writing down the name of the first animal called out. Write this animal's name on every piece of paper.

After 12 animals have been shouted out, fold up each piece of paper and put them in your container. So, now you have 12 pieces of paper in the basket with the same animal's name written on each piece. But the audience thinks there are 12 different animals' names on the pieces of paper.

Now tell everyone that you are going to predict which animal will be pulled out of the basket by a member of the audience. Concentrate very hard and then write the same animal's name as before on a blank piece of paper.

Seal the piece of paper in an envelope and give it to a member of the audience to hold.

Now ask another member of the audience to pick any piece of paper out of the basket, unfold it and read out the animal's name written on it.

TIGER!

Now ask the person with the envelope to open it and read what is written on the piece of paper inside. Incredibly, as far as your audience is concerned, it will be the same animal.

TIGER!

Oh yes, I remember doing this one in Las Vegas. How they cheered and cheered.

So that's animal magic for you. It's certainly time we stopped rabbiting on about it and let you get on with the rest of the book...

CURIOUS CARDS

In England in the 1930s, a young amateur magician approached the brilliant David Devant, boasting that he knew 300 card tricks. He wanted to know how many tricks Devant knew. Devant fixed the young man with a serious stare and answered the question.

What do you think he said? Was it:

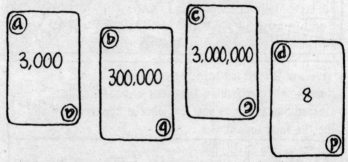

The answer was d) 8, and this is a crucial fact for anyone interested in the wonders of card magic. There are only a certain number of tricks you can perform with cards – it's *how* you perform them that is so vital. You need quick hands and a quick mind. You also need quick feet if everything goes wrong and you need to make a speedy getaway. A pack of cards is one of the most crucial elements in a magician's box of tricks. After all, with 52 cards and two jokers, the possibilities for mind-boggling magic are endless.

You want to freak out your friends and fool your family? Then pack in whatever you're doing and prepare for some tips on becoming a card genius.

The birth of cards

Playing cards have been around for centuries and, since the Chinese invented paper, it's no surprise to discover that they were the first to produce a pack. But it wasn't until the 1300s that the first packs of cards arrived in Europe. It's not known who introduced them, but it's possible that crusader knights may have brought them back from the Middle East.

At that time, society was split into four main classes of people: the Church, the military, the merchants and the farmers. The playing cards reflected these social classes and were divided into four picture groups:

CUPS- REPRESENTING THE CHURCH

SWORDS- REPRESENTING THE MILITARY

FIVE- POINTED STAR- REPRESENTING MERCHANTS

BATONS- REPRESENTING FARMERS

But these early packs of cards weren't much good for doing tricks because...

1. They were printed on very thick paper and were difficult to handle

2. They were very large.

3. They were very expensive. The only people who ever got their hands on playing cards were those with stacks of money.

By the 1500s, as printing costs went down, much smaller and cheaper versions of cards were being produced. The modern "suits" that we still use today appeared – red hearts and diamonds, black clubs and spades. Magicians were delighted with these new packs because now the cards fitted easily into their hands. This made the performance of tricks a good deal easier.

Sensational Soma

Around this time, an Italian by the name of Girolamo Cordano witnessed the amazing tricks of a young card magician by the name of Francesco Soma. He described one particular trick in which Soma spread a pack of cards face down. An audience member took a card and hid it. Soma shuffled the pack and, without looking at any of the cards, he announced what the missing card was. Then he asked for the card to be put back in the pack and told several people to pick out a card, before returning it to the pack. Every person picked out the originally chosen card. Cordano couldn't figure out how Soma's tricks worked. Perhaps it was a special pack where all of the cards were exactly the same. Whatever the secret of Soma's magic, Cordano concluded that his tricks were "too wonderful". They might seem simple enough to us today, but at the time, they were very new and exciting.

Tricks of the trade - stooges and confederates

Sometimes, magicians will choose an audience member to assist them with a card trick. However, this isn't always a random choice. Unknown to the rest of the audience, the person chosen is "in on the act" and is secretly helping the magician with the trick. Known as stooges and confederates, these people are often used by card magicians and as part of a host of other magical feats.

Other cards to note

Over the next few hundred years, interest in card magic spread like wildfire throughout Europe. Soon, in all of the salons and dining halls of Europe, people were begging for card tricks. The best magicians were able to book big theatres and charge people money for the benefit of seeing their craft – and their tricks became even more marvellous. In the 1700s:

● A poster for Isaac Fawkes' performance (remember him?) boasted that he would demonstrate a trick whereby a pack of cards would be flung high into the air and would transform itself into a collection of live birds.

● An English magician called Ingleby asked a man in the room to hold a pack of cards in his hand and think of a particular card. When the man had thought of a card, Ingleby asked him to throw the whole pack of cards at him. The cards were thrown with full force and Ingleby caught one card in his mouth. To the marvel of everyone in the room, the card was the one selected by the man.

58

- In one performance, the great Italian magic maestro Pinetti asked someone to choose a card, replace it in the pack and shuffle the cards. He then produced a gun and fired a bullet into the air. The bullet whizzed across the stage and lodged itself into a wall of the theatre. Amazingly, the card that a member of the audience had chosen was pinned to the wall, shot right though by the bullet. Some claimed that Pinetti used a special pack where all the cards were identical but that still didn't explain the firing part of the trick. Pinetti got quite a name for himself and on one occasion performed at the court of Marie Antoinette and Louis XVI in France.

So how are all these brilliant tricks actually done? What all card magicians have in common is a great determination to practise and a selection of brilliant hand movements. Before we look at some of the best-known tricks in the business, let's have a look at some of these crucial card-magic skills...

Tricks of the trade

Forcing – making someone choose a particular card whilst they think they are choosing it of their own free will. Sometimes, this can be as simple as jutting out one card in the pack a little further than all of the others. Sounds too good to be true? Well, try it and see!

Palming – taking a card in one of your hands and hiding it there without the audience knowing. This can be a problem if you have very small hands! If you look very closely at some card magicians on TV, you can see that during or at the end of a trick, one of their fists is clenched, concealing a card or set of cards.

The pass – bringing a card from one position in the pack to another without the audience seeing – perhaps from the middle to the top of the pack.

Flourishes – movements that you want the audience to see. Sometimes, these are just for effect but at other times they aim to focus the attention of the audience away from something else you're doing, for example, dramatically fanning a pack of cards with one hand whilst secretly hiding a card in your other hand. This type of flourish is a classic piece of misdirection.

Marking – secretly placing a mark on a card before or during a trick so that you can easily locate that card. A tiny pen mark or slight bend in a card's corner may be all that you need to find that card.

False shuffle – appearing to shuffle a pack of cards, whilst keeping a card or cards in a certain place. By moving a pack of cards very fast up and down on to the palm of one hand, you can sometimes create the illusion of shuffling, whilst in reality no cards have moved anywhere!

LOOK! A MONSTER!

WHERE?

WHY HAS IT GOT 'THIS ONE' WRITTEN ON THE BACK?

SHUFFLE, SHUFFLE, SHUFFLE, SHUFFLE...

Legendary card tricks

Now you've been introduced to some of the tricks of the trade, it's time to look at some of the best card tricks of all time and some of the people who invented them...

1. An ace in the pack

Nate Leipzig was one of the world's greatest card magicians. Originally from Sweden he rose to great fame in the USA in the early 1900s. One of his favourite tricks involved asking four audience members to put the four aces into different parts of a pack. When he revealed the four cards at the top of the pack, these were the four aces. They'd miraculously risen to the top of the pack.

Leipzig's most spectacular trick involved two chosen cards being replaced in a pack, which was then shuffled. Next, with utmost drama, Leipzig wrapped the whole pack in newspaper. With a knife in one hand and the pack in the other, he stabbed through the paper into the side of the pack. Miraculously, when the newspaper was pulled away, the knife was between the two chosen cards. To achieve this effect, Leipzig may have used a false shuffle, but no one can be sure.

2. The rising-card trick

In the late 1800s, Howard Thurston began performing the Rising Card Trick. A selection of chosen cards appeared to float up from a pack on a table into Thurston's hand. Some audience members claimed that he must have used wires, but no one ever saw them.

3. The three-card trick

This is a classic trick involving a magician showing an audience three cards – often two cards of the same black suit and a queen from a red suit. The magician places the queen or "lady" in between the other two cards for all to see, then lays the three cards face down on the surface. Members of the audience are invited to bet on where they think the "lady" is. More often than not they're wrong, because magicians use sleight of hand to make the queen vanish. The people betting lose their money and the magician is a bit richer.

YOU'LL HAVE TO MOVE ON, SIR, BUT BEFORE YOU DO, I'LL HAVE FIVE POUNDS ON THAT CARD.

HUH?

4. The six-card trick

In the early 1900s, the British magician Elis Stanyon invented the remarkable six-card repeat. He didn't achieve much fame with the trick himself but, in the 1930s, American Tommy Tucker did. The trick involves the magician holding six cards in the air. Three of the cards are thrown away. The cards remaining in the magician's hands are counted and it soon becomes clear that there aren't three but six cards there. It seems pretty likely that in this trick the magician palms an extra three cards away from the prying eyes of the audience.

5. The games man

One of the great magic spectacles of the 1900s was provided by card genius Lionel King. He selected four members from the audience and seated them around a card table. Breaking the seal on a brand-new pack, he dealt the cards out for a game of whist. King then moved to the back of the theatre and called out directions for the players. Even though it was completely impossible for him to see the cards, he directed the whole game as if he could see everyone's cards.

THE STUPID-LOOKING MAN TO GO NEXT...

HE MEANS YOU.

ME?

Many observers were sure that one of the game players was a stooge of King's, and was somehow letting him know which cards everyone was holding, but this wasn't proven.

6. The Green party

One night in the middle of the World War II, the British Prime Minister Winston Churchill was completely spooked by some card magic. A magician called Harry Green showed Churchill a trick called "Out of this world".

Green took a red and a black card and placed them face up a few centimetres away from each other. He then handed Churchill the rest of the pack. He told the prime minister to deal every card in the rest of the pack face down on to the red card or the black card. Churchill was instructed not to look at any of the cards, but to "imagine" as he dealt them whether they were red or black.

Churchill, thinking it impossible to deal all red and black cards on to the right piles without seeing them, did as he was told. When he'd dealt the fiftieth card, Green triumphantly picked up the piles to reveal all of the red cards in the red pile and all of the black cards in the black pile. Churchill was so bowled over by the trick that he demanded Green repeat it several times, late into the night.

65

One theory about this amazing trick was that Green palmed two piles of cards – one red pile and one black. When he picked up the piles Churchill had dealt, he swapped them for the prepared, palmed piles that he had in his hands.

Blaine on the street

Modern street magician David Blaine's remarkable repertoire includes two particularly brilliant pieces of card magic. In one, he asks a member of the public to select a card. Blaine looks away and asks the passer-by to show the card to the TV camera. Blaine then asks for the card to be returned to the pack. Immediately, the magic man throws the pack against a shop window. All of the cards fall to the floor apart from one. You've guessed it – the chosen card. This card is stuck to the glass of the shop window. And if you think that's amazing, there's more, because the card isn't stuck to the outside of the glass window, it's stuck to the inside!

Another Blaine trick involves asking someone to pick a card and replace it in the pack. Blaine then tells them that the card is under the person's foot. The person looks under their shoe and there's nothing there. So Blaine tells them to take off the shoe. Sure enough the card has ended up inside it!

Blaine never spills the beans on any of his tricks, but many people insist that he must use stooges to help create his brilliant illusions.

Is all of this card magic making you want to get in on the act? No problem. The Great Miraculo is standing by with a little number of his own.

A salty solution

For this wonderful card trick, all you need is a pack of cards, a magic wand – if you don't have a wand use a pencil – a table and a few grains of ordinary household salt. Clumsini, salt please!

I said 'a few grains', Clumsini.

Select a member of your audience. Ask them to pick a card from the pack you're holding in your hand. Then ask them to remember this card and hold on to it.

HMM...

Tell the audience member that they must cut the pack, then put the two halves of the pack face down on the table in front of you.

Point to one of the halves of the pack and ask them to place their chosen card face down on top of this half.

As carefully as you can, secretly drop the grains of salt on top of the chosen card. You can use a well-practised flourish here to distract the audience. Then place the other half of the pack on top. Hold the whole pack together with one hand.

Announce to the audience that by a simple tap of your wand (or pencil) you will magically be able to separate the pack at the exact place where the chosen card has been left.

68

Say the magic word – Cardlicious! – let go of the pack and, as you do so, tap gently on the top of it. The grains of salt will make the top half slide off. You can then turn over the top card of the bottom half of the pack, which will of course be the chosen card.

The person who chose the card will scream with delight and the audience will become hoarse with cheering. Take a well-deserved bow and make sure that no one sees the grains of salt.

Double bluff

Modern American performers Penn and Teller keep on shocking the magic world because they reveal to TV audiences how many of their tricks are done. But, on one occasion, they double-bluffed everyone. Penn stood in a street and got a member of the public to pick a card from a pack he was holding and keep it out of his sight. Then Penn fanned the rest of the pack and suddenly announced what the chosen card was.

How did they do that?
Penn and Teller's card trick

Teller was sitting in a TV studio and explained to the watching millions that he had operated a special camera to help Penn find the missing card. The camera, he said, studied the fanned cards in Penn's hand and immediately picked out which one was missing. Teller then spoke this information into a microphone linked to an earpiece that Penn was wearing. Penn could thus declare the identity of the missing card. TV audiences were impressed by this clever feat. But it was all big lie.

PENN TELLER

How did they **really** do that?

There was no special camera to study the fanned cards. Penn had simply "forced" a card on to an unsuspecting member of the public and so knew all along what the card was. The joke was on the TV audience, who had believed Teller's tale about a brilliant piece of modern gadgetry, whilst in reality Penn was simply using one of the oldest tricks in the book. In the end, of course, they told the audience the whole truth – as they often do to the annoyance of many other magicians.

To become a great card magician takes hour after hour of hard work and dedicated practice. But if you do crack it, there's nothing more satisfying than seeing the faces of an audience who've been completely bamboozled by a superb card trick. And remember, as David Devant said at the beginning of this chapter, you only need eight basic card tricks to have the makings of a great show...

DRAMATIC DISAPPEARANCES

The Vanishing Act is one of the finest pieces of entertainment in any magician's repertoire. The art of making something disappear into thin air has been baffling and bemusing audiences for centuries but it wasn't until the 1600s that vanishing really took off. It was thanks mainly to something called a codpiece...

A codpiece was a large piece of material that covered up the opening in the front of men's breeches. Audiences would believe that a magician had made an object vanish when in fact it had ended up in his codpiece.

I KNEW I SHOULDN'T HAVE MADE THAT HEDGEHOG DISAPPEAR!

By the 1700s, magicians had begun to use tables to perform their vanishing tricks. These folding tables contained a small hidden bag known as a servante. The magician could pull up and push down the bag without the audience seeing, and it served as a perfect hiding place for objects.

Now you see it, now you don't

Disappearing acts began to grow in popularity and by the 1800s, magicians were making people vanish rather than just objects. They had devised ever more cunning and inventive ways to fool their audiences. Here's a selection of them:

The magic palanquin

In this performance, four men carry onstage a carriage called a palanquin that rests on two poles. Inside the carriage, a woman sits beneath a small canopy. An assistant walks onstage and draws a set of curtains around the woman. Moments later the assistant pulls the curtains back. To the astonishment of the audience the lady has vanished.

The magic secret – The canopy is painted very cleverly to make it look much smaller than it really is. As the curtains are closed, the woman climbs up inside the canopy and lies hiding there when the curtains are opened.

Disappearing lady

For this stunt the magician places a newspaper on the stage floor. A lady is covered with a cloth as she sits on a chair on top of the newspaper. The magician holds up the cloth and, with a sudden movement, he pulls back the cloth to reveal that the woman has disappeared.

The magic secret – A special hole has been cut in the newspaper that corresponds exactly with the size of a stage trapdoor. The newspaper is laid down with its hole over the trapdoor. As the magician is holding up the cloth, the lady climbs down through the hole in the newspaper and through the trapdoor. She can also reappear when needed. The magician has an uncut newspaper to hand to show to the audience at the end of the trick, whilst secretly hiding the cut newspaper.

Vanity fair

A person stands with their back to the audience in front of a mirror. The magician covers them and the mirror with a cloth and tells the audience that very soon the person will vanish. The magician pulls back the cloth and the person is nowhere to be seen.

The magic secret – The mirror is a trick one with a special hole cut in its surface near the bottom. As soon as the person is covered by the cloth, a piece of movable glass is levered up by an assistant backstage. The person is then able to climb feet first through the hole. Using this clever device, the person can also be made to reappear.

You think you can make an object vanish? Well, good for you! All you need to do now is convince an audience. As always, this can be done with the help of the Great Miraculo himself.

All you need to perform this trick is a small coin, a matchbox and a knife. Oh, and an adult to help with the knife.

Ask the adult to cut three little slits in one end of the matchbox drawer, like so. This way you create a little flap. Clumsini is performing this task for me.

Great work, Clumsini. Now, put the matchbox drawer back inside the matchbox.

You are now ready for the act! Hold the matchbox up in one hand and the coin in your other hand, so that the audience can see them both. Tell them that you are going to make the coin vanish.

Push open the uncut end of the matchbox drawer in full view of the audience and drop the coin inside. Close the matchbox drawer and rattle the box so they can hear that the coin is definitely in there.

RATTLE!

Now, very carefully, turn your hand away from the audience and let the coin slip out through the cut end of the drawer. This is the most important part of the trick, so practise it over and over until you get it right. When you have the coin in your hand, hold it firmly and make sure that the flap is closed. You can use your thumb to do this.

Dramatically take the matchbox with your free hand and hold it high in the air. As you do this, secretly drop the coin from your other hand into a pocket. Say the magic word – Vanishenzi! – and shake the matchbox.

DROP COIN

The audience will be baffled, because they will hear no rattling sound. Very carefully, push open the uncut drawer and show the audience the empty matchbox. You have made the coin disappear!

If you want to be really clever, you can make the coin appear again. You do this by using a classic piece of misdirection. Say that you have finished with the matchbox, shake it in the air with one hand and then throw it backwards over your shoulder.

As the audience is watching you throw the matchbox, quickly pull out the coin from your pocket with your other hand. Hold it tightly so that no one can see it. It is then up to you where you want the coin to appear again. You can walk over to an audience member and pretend to pull it from behind their ear or reach up to a book on a bookshelf and pull it out from there.

Victorious vanishers

Nowadays magicians have become more ambitious and seem to be able to make just about anything disappear no matter how big or how impossible. Here's a selection of the biggest and best feats...

● Possibly the most incredible disappearing stunt ever performed happened in 1981 when American superstar magician David Copperfield made an aeroplane disappear. (Some magicians might argue about this being the most incredible stunt ever, but no one had attempted anything like this before and it certainly started a craze for making massive things disappear).

With millions watching on TV, Copperfield got a large group of volunteers to circle the plane and hold hands. (As you'll see elsewhere in this book, there are many who believe that Copperfield's "volunteers" are really in on the act.) These people were then surrounded by a series of giant screens. The television audience could still see the silhouette of the plane as the magician and his team used brilliant lighting effects. As dramatic and loud music was played to drown out their noises, Copperfield's assistants wheeled the plane away. With a wave of his hands, Copperfield asked for the screens to be pulled back and to the astonishment of the TV audience, the plane was gone.

● In 1985, magician Meir Yedid appeared on Paul Daniels's magic show in Britain and amazed everyone by making his fingers vanish.

● Paul Daniels himself pulled off an amazing feat

of magic when he made one of the cameras recording his television show disappear, much to the astonishment of the cameraman!

● In 1986, one-time president of the Magic Circle (a British magic society that many of the world's top magicians belong to), David Berglas got two nurses to hold his wrists and take his pulse. They kept holding on to his wrists as he made his pulse "disappear".

● One of Siegfried and Roy's most famous tricks is making an elephant disappear. Not a toy baby elephant though, a real live fully grown elephant. And the truly amazing thing about this illusion is the speed at which it happens. Within moments of the elephant going into a box, it's gone. That's one trick the elephant will never forget!

...AND FOR MY NEXT TRICK.

● In 1994, Franz Harary went one better than David Copperfield by making a NASA Space Shuttle Explorer disappear. Of course, NASA wouldn't have been too happy if he hadn't given it back, so moments later he made it reappear!

The magicians who perform these amazing illusions are very secretive about how they're done. Sometimes they even get their assistants to sign contracts saying that they promise never to tell anyone. But, if you promise to keep it very quiet we can reveal how some magicians make very large things disappear…

How did they do that?
Making very large objects disappear

1. More often than not, the magician shows the object that is going to vanish…

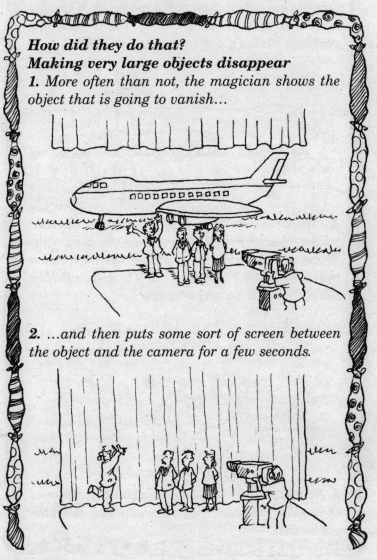

2. …and then puts some sort of screen between the object and the camera for a few seconds.

3. The screen is then taken away and, incredibly, the object has disappeared. What actually happens is that the magician, the screen and the camera are all on a movable platform. When the screen is placed in front of the object, the platform moves a few metres to one side.

4. We aren't aware of this as the camera, magician and screen all move at the same time in exactly the same way, giving the impression that they haven't moved at all. The screen is then lifted to reveal an empty space.

5. Sometimes, a live audience actually witnesses these feats. However, they are usually all in on the act as well.

If all of these magicians continue confounding us with bigger and better vanishing acts, who knows where it all might end?

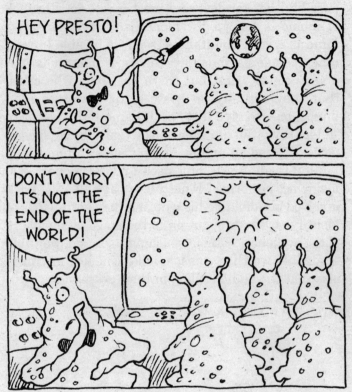

MYSTERIOUS MENTALISM

Possibly the weirdest and most mysterious branch of magic is known as "mentalism". Performers of mind magic or "mentalists" seem to be able to read other people's minds. For the most part, it is just a very clever trick, but there are some who claim that they actually *do* possess the power to read minds, or – to give it its posh name – the power of "telepathy". But do mentalists really have special powers? Read on and make up your own mind...

Mind-reading was first used in 1784 as part of a magic act performed Pinetti (see page 59). His trick involved blindfolding his wife and then getting her to identify objects brought on to the stage by members of the audience. Without touching them, she was able to identify watches, coins, handkerchiefs or anything else that the audience had in their possession.

IS IT A WOOLLY JUMPER?

The secret of the Pinettis' trick remains unknown, but it is possible that he and his wife used code words to identify different objects, a bit like this next couple...

It's a mindfield

Julius Zancig and his wife Agnes performed in the late 1800s and early 1900s. They billed themselves as "two minds with but a single thought," and their act involved Agnes reading Julius's mind to find out information about members of the audience. Observers were amazed and astonished at what seemed to be an incredible act of telepathy, but in reality Julius and Agnes used a complicated series of code words...

How did they do that?
The Zancigs' mind-reading trick

In the Zancigs' code, one word could have many different meanings. For example, the word, please had seven different meanings. It could mean the letter F, the month of June, the number 6, a post-office worker, Friday, the names Frank or Francis and a telegram or letter.

For example, if Julius said, "I have been handed an object by a gentleman. Please tell me his name", then Agnes would know that the man's name was Frank. Similarly, the word, but meant the letter S, the number 19 and pipe cleaner. The word give meant watch and 9. So, if Julius said,

PLEASE TELL ME, BOB'S NAME...

BOB

"But, please give me the names of three articles I am holding", Agnes would know that he was holding a pipe cleaner, a letter and a watch. Julius came from Denmark – if his language seemed a little odd at times, audiences just thought it was because of that.

So, if Julius said, *"Please, but, please give me the numbers on this piece of paper"*, what number would he be trying to tell Agnes? Now you know their secret code, you should be able to work it out.

Answer: 61969

The Pinettis and the Zancigs were double-act mentalists, but audiences back then quickly worked out a lot of their codes. Soon, they wanted something new and truly incredible to impress them. In the 1920s, a magician burst on to the scene who was determined to perform mind magic on his own – without the help of an assistant.

Mind-blowing magic

Calling himself the president of the American Psychical Society, Joseph Dunninger had a very powerful and mysterious presence. In 1920, he put on a show in Boston in which he asked five members of the audience to write words on pieces of paper. An assistant collected these pieces of paper and put them in an envelope. For safe keeping, the assistant put the envelope on the floor and put his foot on it. Dunninger, concentrating hard, then proceeded to guess correctly what was on each piece of paper.

As well as being an amazing mentalist, Dunninger was also very good at gaining publicity for himself, often using his magical abilities when faced with a tricky situation.

On one occasion, Dunninger's car was stolen. When he reported the theft to the police they laughed and said, "Why don't you tell us who stole it and where it is?" So Dunninger thought about it for a while and then told the police that he didn't know who had stolen it, but he knew it was in Yorkville (a district of New York City). Incredibly, when the police searched in Yorkville, they found Dunninger's car smashed against a pillar. Some people thought Dunninger had set this up and taken his car there himself, but, when the police found the car, they also found professional car thief Robert Cunningham in it. He probably felt a bit telepathetic.

Dunninger soon became a very successful magician, first on radio and then on television where he had a show on all three of America's channels. His act continued to amaze people especially a feature he named "Brain Busters".

Dunninger would read the minds of people who were outside the television studio. In fact, not only were they outside the studio, often they were deep under the ocean in a submarine or high above the clouds in an aeroplane. During one show, he even opened a locked safe in America's National Jewellery Exchange by reading the thoughts of the two guards, each of whom knew half of the combination. (They were in two minds about appearing on the show.)

Speaking his mind

Dunninger's envelope trick became so popular that magic shops started selling explanations of how they thought it was done. Unfortunately, the shops hadn't asked for Dunninger's permission and so, in 1927, in a magazine called, *Science and Invention*, he wrote the following:

> *Many dealers in magical equipment are charging exorbitant prices for this effect claiming it is the method I use. To prove it is not, I am disclosing the system forthwith.*

He then went on to describe exactly how he did the trick...

How did they do that?
Dunninger's envelope trick

1. Dunninger's assistants would hand out slips of paper to members of the audience.

2. Dunninger would ask the audience members to write some information on the slips, such as their name, address or date of birth, and then get them to fold the slips of paper over several times so that what they had written could not be seen.

3. Dunninger and his assistants would then ask the audience to put their slips of paper into envelopes that they were handing round.

4. It is at this point that some of the slips, when handed to Dunninger or one of his assistants, were palmed and replaced by blank slips of paper. The blank slips of paper were placed inside the envelopes.

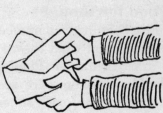

5. *Using misdirection, the palmed slips were secretly read so that their contents could be later revealed to the audience.*

Apart from this one time, Dunninger never revealed the secrets behind his amazing abilities, but he did make a few mysterious comments about them. He once said, "Any child of 12 could do what I do, with 30 years of practice." He also referred to what he did as, "telasthesia", and said, "You pick up a vivid impression from another mind and others follow or suggest themselves. But it isn't mind reading; it is thought reading." Confused? That's probably what Dunninger wanted people to be...

Food for thought

Since Dunninger, a number of other mentalists have claimed that what they do involves "real" telepathy – in particular, the Piddingtons, a husband and wife double act who were seemingly able to transmit information to each other over long distances. On one occasion in 1949, Lesley Piddington was locked up in the Tower of London whilst her husband, Sidney, successfully transmitted information to her from a television studio far away. Mysteriously, they never explained how they did their tricks and would end their show by saying, "Telepathy or not telepathy? You are the judge."

In certain mentalist tricks, information is revealed by the magician *after* the volunteer has given it. For example, the mentalist writes something down on a piece of paper and seals it in an envelope. He then asks someone in the audience to think of their cat's name. The mentalist concentrates very hard before asking the person to say what their cat's name is. The magician *then* rips open the envelope to reveal a piece of paper on which is written the cat's name is written.

In this case the mentalist may be using a "nail writer"…

Tricks of the trade – the nail writer

1. The nail writer is a tiny ring that fits on to a finger. On the end of this ring is an even tinier piece of pencil lead or a even a really, really small pen.

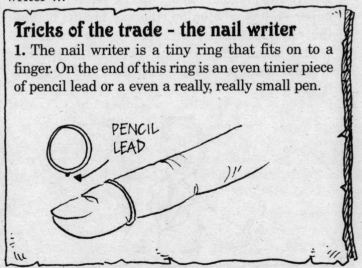

PENCIL
LEAD

2. Once the audience member has revealed their secret information, such as the name of their cat, the mentalist uses misdirection so that he can secretly and quickly write the cat's name down on a second piece of paper hidden behind the envelope, using his nail writer.

3. The magician then rips open the envelope and pretends to take out the piece of paper inside. Really, the magician holds up the second piece of paper he has written on (the one hidden behind the envelope) and shows this to the audience, whilst scrunching up the envelope (with the original blank piece of paper inside) and throwing it away.

Muscling in on the act

Another group of mentalists perform what is known as muscle-reading, or contact mind-reading. The crucial thing about this technique is that the performer has to have some physical contact with the person whose mind they're reading. Often this means holding hands, but it can involve hand-to-shoulder contact or even being connected by holding the opposite ends of a handkerchief.

The first person to bring muscle-reading to the public was John Randall Brown towards the end of the 1800s. He claimed to have discovered the skill whilst playing hunt the thimble as a child – he probably held hands with the person who'd hidden the thimble and found it every time. Bet he wasn't much fun to play with!

In Brown's act, he would ask a member of the audience to hide a pin anywhere in the theatre – it could be hidden in a shoe, down the back of a chair or in the ladies loo.

Wherever it was, Brown would hold the hand of the person who had hidden it and – without saying a word – lead that person back to the pin.

More recently, a Hungarian muscle-reader called Franz J Polgar developed the technique. He was able to find a small silver banknote clip that had been hidden somewhere in New York's Empire State Building, an office building with 102 floors. Can you imagine finding that? It would be like trying to find a tiny needle in the biggest haystack in the world.

Polgar would finish his act by playing a very risky game of hide-and-seek with the audience – risky for him, that is, because what was being hidden was his pay cheque. If he didn't find it, he said that he would leave the theatre without his wages. Over the years, the audience hid Polgar's money in some very odd places – the hollowed-out heel of a shoe, sealed in a tennis ball ... they even hid it in the barrel of a policeman's gun. But Polgar always found his money.

How did they do that?
Muscle-reading (contact mind-reading)
Some of the secrets of contact mind-reading were revealed by the famous Nobel-prize-winning physicist, Richard Feynman. In his biography, he remembers, as a young child, seeing a

mind-reader find a five-dollar note that had been hidden somewhere in Feynman's town. The mind-reader took the hand of the person who had hidden the note and began walking through the town, "reading their thoughts." He found it in a drawer in someone's house. Afterwards, Richard's father asked the mind-reader how he did it. This is what he told him.

The mind reader explained that you hold on to their hands, loosely, and as you move, you jiggle a little bit. You come to an intersection, you jiggle a little bit to the left, and if it's incorrect you feel a certain amount of resistance, because they don't expect you to move that way. But when you move in the right direction, because they think you might be able to do it, they give way more easily and there's no resistance. So you must always be jiggling a bit, testing out which seems to be the easiest way.

If you want to try this out, it's best to have the person whose mind you're reading on your left side, about one pace behind you. Good luck!

Still mental

Mind magic is as popular today as it ever was and still as controversial. Israeli-born Uri Geller is one person who performs mental feats and maintains that he uses only the power of his mind. He's best known for bending spoons by using what he says is "psychokinesis" – the ability to move or affect objects with your mind.

Uri is also famous for making people's watches and clocks stop or start for no apparent reason. Often when he appears on television, people who are watching find that a clock that hasn't worked for years suddenly starts working again. Geller also performs mind-reading feats and has attempted to influence things like the outcome of football matches by using the power of positive thought. He has done this by putting crystals that he claims give off positive energy into the goal before a big international football match. He also asked people to touch a ball that appeared on a television screen and to think positively about the winning team. Unfortunately, these attempts have not always proved successful. But this is what he says about his "powers":

> *I don't very much care if you think I'm a fake. After 30 years of proving my powers, and at least 11,000 bent spoons, I am used to sceptics* [people who don't believe in his powers]. *Many people would prefer to call me a liar than to admit that they might have been wrong about the paranormal.*

However, magicians say that they can do all of the things that Uri Geller does using magic techniques and it has been noted that a spoon-bending effect did appear in the magic magazine *Abracadabra* some time before Uri Geller's public performances. In fact there is even a book, *Gellerism Revealed* by Ben Harris that claims to explain all of what he does. But the fact remains that to this day, no one is really sure.

Another world-famous mentalist around today is Max Maven. He was once described as "the most original mind in magic", and listed as one of the 100 most influential people in magic. He claims that he can tell what a person is thinking, no matter what language they speak.

Maven is not afraid to use modern technology and has created a number of interactive effects, including a holograph of a 20-cm (eight-inch) wizard called "Maximus Maven" that performs mind-reading tricks on members of the public.

All we can tell you about Max Maven's feats is that he uses very clever psychological techniques to "get inside people's heads".

By now, you're probably going out of your mind wanting to find out how to do a mentalist trick for yourself. Well, you don't need to be a mind-reader to know who's about to show you how it's done. Yes, it's the Great Miraculo.

Hello, hello. So you want to know how to do a mind-reading trick, eh? Ah yes, I remember that I once read the mind of a hyena. Oh, it did make me laugh. Anyway, for this trick, all you'll need are some cards and a friend. Clumsini – ten cards, please, and make sure a number-ten card is amongst them!

Thank you, Clumsini. Right, now it's very important that you lay the cards out like this, just like the symbols on a number ten card.

Now, turn your back, leave the room or put a blindfold on. Then ask a member of the audience to point to one of the cards.

Come back to the cards and explain that your friend from the audience is going to touch the cards and, as they do so, you are going to pick up vibrations from their mind so that you can tell which card was chosen.

In case the audience thinks you and your friend have already decided how many times to touch the cards, you must say that you are going to ask someone for a number. This number will be the number of times that your friend touches the card.

Once someone has given you a number, all you have to do is watch carefully as your friend touches the cards with a finger. You see, it doesn't matter how many times the cards are touched, but it does matter where they are touched. In particular, where the number-ten card is touched.

The cards are laid out in the same way as the symbols on the ten card. So, if your friend touches the ten card here, you'll know that the chosen card is in that position.

Right, that's that finished. Time to clear everything away, Clumsini!

So that's mentalism. Whatever you think about it, it's probably best to keep an open mind...

FLOATING AROUND

A length of rope that uncoils itself? A violin flying around a room? People floating in mid-air without support? Do you want to find out how these stupendous acts of wonder work? Well, before we let you in on a few trade secrets, let's take a look at where it all started...

Traveller's tales

In the 1200s, lots of people started to get bitten by the travel bug, thanks to legendary explorer Marco Polo, famed for his travels in the Far East. Many followed in his footsteps and, like him, they began reporting on a series of amazing magical feats taking place in India. Some of these stunts involved making objects or people float in the air without any visible support – a process known as "levitation".

DON'T GET CARRIED AWAY!

These levitation tricks were often demonstrated by Indian spiritual men known as fakirs. Many tales of the fakirs' amazing powers were told, but there was one that referred to a particularly astonishing spectacle. This is how observers described it...

1. A series of burning torches were lit and placed near the audience. On the ground lay a long coil of rope and a woven basket.

2. Before the fakir began the trick, a boy played a flute and the fakir beat a drum. The boy then dragged the coil of rope over to where the fakir was playing his drum. The fakir carried on playing and the audience waited.

3. After a while, the rope suddenly began to rise off the ground. Its coils slowly unwound until it was fully extended and stretched out in the air.

4. The fakir then threw some incense into the torches and great billows of smoke drifted out over the rope. He clicked his fingers and the boy started to climb up the rope, disappearing into the smoke.

5. After a few minutes the fakir asked the boy to come down but the boy didn't answer. The fakir called again but still there was no reply. Appearing to be very angry the fakir then started to climb the rope himself in search of the boy. He reappeared some moments later and told the audience that the boy had vanished.

6. As the fakir stood in front of the audience, shouting was heard from inside the woven basket. The fakir walked over to the basket, pulled off its lid and out jumped the boy. The audience applauded loudly. The fakir and the boy took a series of majestic bows.

Magic history is full of people who have proclaimed that this Indian Rope Trick revealed truly magical powers. In 1355, an Arab who called himself Ibn Batutu (the traveller) claimed that on a trip to China he'd been in the audience when the Indian Rope Trick was performed. And, in the 1800s, writer Maxim Gorky said that he'd seen the trick first-hand. Both men really believed that they had witnessed a truly magical feat.

In the 1600s, Indian ruler Jahangir reported seeing some magicians from Bengal throwing a long chain into the air. It stayed up, extended to its full length. The magician called over to a selection of animals and, one by one, a dog, a hog, a panther, a lion and a tiger each climbed up the chain. When the magician commanded the chain to come back down, none of the animals were anywhere to be seen.

However, in 1954, a collection of Indian men specializing in stage performances decided to look into the matter of the Indian Rope Trick as carefully as they could. They gathered together every piece of evidence that was connected to the trick and examined all of them in the tiniest detail. Then they issued a statement declaring that the Indian Rope Trick was physically impossible and was nothing more than a fascinating fable.

But a year after this famous statement was made someone came forward to reveal the secret of one method behind the illusion. Sadhu Vadramakrishna was an Indian guru who agreed to be interviewed by an American journalist called John Keel. He confessed to Keel that as a young man he'd been involved in performing the Indian Rope Trick and was willing to spill the beans. Here's what he described...

How did they do that?
Sadhu's Indian Rope Trick secrets

- *The fakir and the young boy must be highly trained and very athletic acrobats – the true secret of the trick lies in excellent climbing and balancing skills.*

- *Always perform the trick at night. Make sure the torches on the ground are incredibly bright and shine in the eyes of the audience – making it harder for them to see.*

- *The trick should be staged between two trees or houses and a thin wire must be stretched between them. A light and very thin (and so almost impossible to see) string must be hung over the wire. One end of this string is tied to the end of the coiled rope. The other end is held in the fakir's hand.*

- *When the fakir pulls on the light string the coiled rope appears to rise magically into the smoke-filled air where it remains vertical.*

- *The boy then climbs the rope that is being supported by the fakir who is holding on to the thin length of string – and pulls himself on to the thin wire. Great clouds of smoke are rising over the rope, so the audience can't see the boy when he reaches the top. The boy then ties the rope to the stretched wire and trapeze – walks through the smoke along to one of the trees or houses.*

106

- *The fakir can now climb the rope.*
- *Once back on the ground, the fakir directs the audience's attention towards him. Meanwhile, the boy sneaks down from the tree or house and into the woven basket without the audience seeing him. The fakir then discovers the boy in the basket.*

This confession seemed to explode the whole idea of the mythical Indian Rope Trick. However, in 1999, a certain gentleman arrived on the magic scene and sparked up the debate all over again.

Ishamuddin claimed that he would perform a version of the Indian Rope Trick outside, in full daylight and away from any buildings. Twenty-five thousand people turned up to view this astonishing spectacle. Ishamuddin did appear to make a length of rope rise, from a basket, vertically in the air to about six metres (20 feet). He then got a small boy to climb a short way up the rope. It was a truly remarkable sight and the crowd believed it was magic.

However, some observers insisted that they knew how it was done:

How did they do that?
Ishamuddin's Rope Trick

1. Onlookers claimed that Ishamuddin first showed the crowd a normal length of rope, which he then hid.

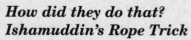

2. Onlookers also said that the "rising" rope was actually wrapped around a length of metal piping, which had been buried in the ground under the basket.

3. An assistant, also hidden beneath the basket, slowly pushed the rope upwards and supported it as the boy climbed on it.

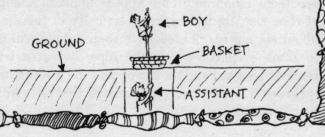

Inspired by the Indian Rope Trick, 19th-century magicians started to levitate all sorts of objects. Some of those early travellers who'd visited India claimed they'd seen humans floating in thin air. Like the Indian Rope Trick, these performances usually featured a fakir or two. Stories passed on by travellers included tales of fakirs who could:

PUT THEMSELVES INTO A TRANCE AND WALK ON AIR.

SOAR INTO THE SKY AND REACH THE MOON.

TRANSFORM THEMSELVES INTO A CUBE, RISE UP INTO THE AIR AND STAY SUSPENDED THERE.

Sheshal's show

In 1830, several European newspapers carried stories about priests floating in mid-air with only a large feather to support them. One of them was able to suspend himself in mid-air with just one elbow resting on a pole. He went by the name of Sheshal.

Sheshal started his show by sitting on a four-legged stool with a bamboo pole poking through it at one end. An assistant held a cloth over Sheshal, whilst he apparently placed himself into a very deep trance. After a few minutes, the assistant pulled back the cloth – and there was Sheshal, suspended 1.2 metres (four feet) in the air, with his elbow resting on the bamboo pole which was now covered by a giant feather. It seemed that Sheshal was floating.

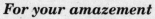

WE'VE BEEN BAMBOO-ZLED!

For your amazement

A Swedish performer by the name of Seeman visited the holy Indian city of Benares in 1872. There he met a fakir called Convinsamy, who appeared to make a young girl float above a flower stand. Convinsamy allowed Seeman to sit very close to this spectacle. The next day, the young girl appeared before Seeman and asked him to follow her. She led him to Convinsamy, whose hands had been scorched by flaming torches. Convinsamy explained that he'd burnt himself as a punishment because he'd let Seeman get too near to a fakir trick and this was strictly forbidden.

Robert-Houdin and his horizontal son

Not to be outdone by their fellow magicians in India, two European men decided to go one – or two – better. In the 1840s, Frenchman Jean-Eugene Robert-Houdin claimed to use a recently discovered gas – called ether – to levitate his son, Emile. The amazed audience believed that the magical ether did the trick.

Then, in London's Crystal Palace, in 1867, an English illusionist called John Nevil Maskelyne appeared to make his wife rise several feet in the air from a standing position.

The Times newspaper commented:

The lady simply rises directly off the floor ... there is no trap.

And Maskelyne's act became even more ambitious. He was able to levitate himself out of a locked cabinet, right above the heads of his audience. Everyone was baffled as to how he achieved this.

An American called Harry Kellar became a keen student of Maskelyne's work and he was determined to find out how the illusionist's tricks were done. He couldn't work them out for himself, so in desperation he resorted to one of the oldest tricks of all – *bribery*. Kellar paid a sum of money to a magician called Paul Valadon who worked for Maskelyne and Valadon promptly revealed the secrets behind the show. Valadon went to work for Kellar in America and it wasn't long before Kellar was producing his own amazing levitation shows, based on Maskelyne's techniques.

Want to know what they were? Oh, all right then. And we'll throw in a few extras too…

Tricks of the trade - levitation

Pole levitation: Many of the most famous illusions of levitation are created by use of a pole hidden in the levitating person's clothing. The person lies on a pole that is connected to a very heavy chair by means of a strong hinge. It appears that the person is floating above the chair, but it is the pole that is supporting their body.

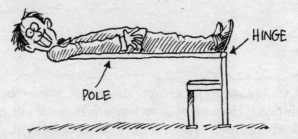

HINGE

POLE

Remember Sheshal and his feather? Well, on closer examination, it was discovered that the vertical pole was actually a length of metal covered with bamboo. When Sheshal was covered with a cloth, his assistant attached a horizontal pole to the top of the vertical pole and covered them both with a giant feather. Sheshal was able to balance on the horizontal pole and create the illusion that he was floating, with only his elbow resting on the horizontal pole.

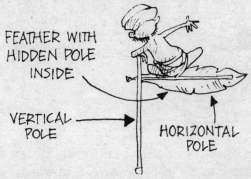

FEATHER WITH HIDDEN POLE INSIDE

VERTICAL POLE

HORIZONTAL POLE

This network of metal poles was probably behind John Nevil Maskelyne's wondrous levitation act.

The false-feet levitation: A person is covered with a sheet so that only their head and feet are sticking out. They then appear to levitate off the ground, with their head and feet still showing at each end of the sheet. In fact, what really happens is that the person has a false set of feet (normally attached to wooden poles) under the sheet.

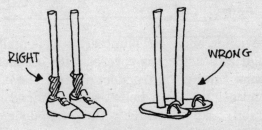

RIGHT

WRONG

The person crouches down and keeps their head showing from one end of the sheet, while holding out the false feet at the other end.

As the sheet is raised up, they straighten their body and move the false feet upwards, thus creating the appearance that their whole body is rising.

The hollow shell: A "Volunteer" (who is really the magician's helper) is covered with a sheet and climbs through a trapdoor in the stage. This volunteer pushes a hollow shell (shaped like a person) up through the trapdoor and underneath the sheet. It appears to the audience that the volunteer is still under the sheet. As the magician lifts the sheet off the ground, they lift the hollow shell as well, to create the illusion that they're levitating the volunteer. When the magician brings the sheet down, the volunteer opens the trapdoor and quickly pulls the hollow shell down. At the same time, the magician whisks the sheet away to reveal that the volunteer has vanished.

HOLLOW SHELL

Levitating legends

Not only does modern magic master David Copperfield levitate around a stage, he also invites a member of the audience to join him for a spot of flying. Copperfield also "flies" inside a cage with a glass roof. One of his assistants walks across this roof to prove that it's solid and that there can be no wires holding the man up. It's a fantastic illusion that has baffled many magic watchers.

Critics of Copperfield claim that he has his own stooges in the first few rows of the audience, so that the real audience can't see any trick wires or ropes. Copperfield, of course, denies such claims, but anyone who works for him does have to sign an agreement that they won't reveal his secrets.

Copperfield pulled off perhaps the greatest levitation illusion of all time when he appeared to float across the massive expanse of the Grand Canyon in Arizona! Although this feat looked very believable, many say that Copperfield simply used all of the tricks of modern trick photography.

David Blaine appears to levitate a few centimetres off the ground in front of passers-by. The act looks incredibly real, but his critics have claimed that he also makes great use of trick photography and special editing techniques in order to present his illusions for a television audience.

Mastering levitation illusions can literally take years of practice and might involve buying some very expensive magic accessories. So here's the Great Miraculo with a simple (and cheap) one to get you started...

Fancy trying your hand at levitation? No problem! You'll need three simple items for this trick:

A small coloured plastic bottle, about 20 cm in length.

A thin piece of rope also about 20 cm in length.

A broken-off piece of a rubber that is a tiny bit smaller than the neck of the bottle.

Clumsini — a bottle, if you please!

Excellent work, Clumsini. I must send you up there more often. Now, before you are ready to show anyone this feat, drop the piece of broken rubber inside the bottle.

Gather an audience together and claim that you possess the power to make a bottle float in mid-air. They will cry "Liar!" and "We don't believe you!" but this is all part of the magician's life, so ignore them.

LIAR!

WE DON'T BELIEVE YOU!

Hold the bottom of the bottle with one hand and place the piece of rope inside the bottle with your other hand. Lift the piece of rope up and down to show that it is not connected to the bottle in any way.

Leave the rope dangling inside the bottle and turn the bottle upside down. As you do this, the piece of rubber will fall to the neck of the bottle and form a wedge with the rope. (You should keep talking to mask the noise the rubber will make.) Make sure the rope is tightly wedged in.

RUBBER

Say the magic word – Floaterama – and turn the bottle back the right way up.

As the bottle is held up the right way, you are holding the rope with one hand and you can take your other hand away from beneath the bottle. Amazingly, the bottle appears to be floating in mid-air with the rope floating inside it!

AXING ASSISTANTS

What would a book about magic be without a chapter on sawing a person in half? Half a book, that's what. Yes, magicians have been decapitating, slicing, severing, cutting, dissecting and snipping bits and pieces off themselves and other people for years. But, until 1921, no one had attempted to chop another person completely in half...

A slice of the action

A man named P T Selbit (real name Percy Tibbles) enjoyed performing all sorts of nasty tricks on his assistants. In the early 1900s, his show included such delights as:

- *The Human Pin Cushion*, in which 84 really sharp spikes appeared to cut through the flesh of his assistant;
- *The Elastic Lady*, where ropes were tied round the ankles and wrists of his assistant and pulled until her arms and legs grew much longer;

I THINK HE'S STRETCHING THIS ACT A BIT TOO FAR!

● *Avoiding the Crush*, in which two assistants in a box were lowered on top of a third assistant who was lying in another box. The third assistant would appear to be crushed flat.

But, on 17 January 1921, Percy performed a trick that was to astonish audiences and send the world of magic reeling. Before a packed audience in London's Finsbury Park Empire, he tied his assistant up with rope and placed her in a large crate. The crate was shut and three sheets of glass plunged through slots in the lid. Two steel blades were also inserted through the crate which, as Selbit pointed out, divided the box into eight very small sections. As if that wasn't enough he then produced a vicious-looking saw and slowly, to increase the tension, proceeded to cut the box in two.

The sheets of glass and the steel blades were then removed and the two halves of the box pulled apart – the assistant's head could be seen sticking out of one half of the box and her feet could be seen sticking out of the other half. In the middle of the two halves was absolutely nothing at all apart from thin air...

To the amazed audience, it looked as if Selbit had chopped straight through his assistant and separated her into two halves. To add even more drama, after the performance Selbit got people to throw buckets of fake blood into the gutters outside the theatre.

So how did Selbit do it? Well, as with a great many tricks, the technique was simple, but very effective:

How did they do that?
Selbit's saw trick

1. The box Selbit used was bottomless and placed on a hollow platform. The assistant got in to the box and let her stomach drop downwards in to the hollow.

2. At the same time, she pushed her head, hands and feet out of the ends of the box. Selbit then sawed through the box down to the platform and inserted slabs so that the sections could be separated.

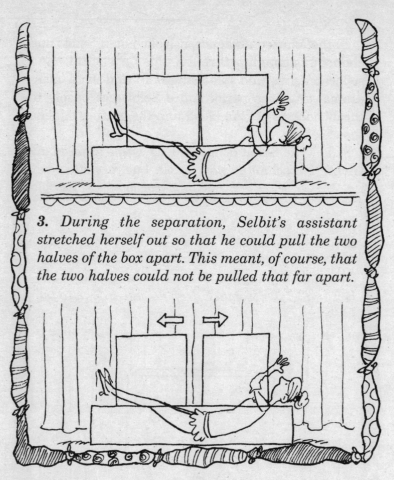

3. *During the separation, Selbit's assistant stretched herself out so that he could pull the two halves of the box apart. This meant, of course, that the two halves could not be pulled that far apart.*

Selbit's trick was an instant hit, but that's only half the story. A few months later, a magician in New York City called Horace Goldin started doing his own version of the trick. In Goldin's performance, the box was much bigger and, once he'd sawn through it, he sealed each half with a metal blade and pulled them much further apart than in Selbit's trick. So how did Goldin do it?

How did they do that?
Goldin's saw trick

1. In this method two assistants were used. One went into the box whilst the other one was hidden in the hollow platform under the box.

2. After the lid was closed, the assistant in the box pulled her knees up so that she only occupied one half of the box.

3. The first assistant then pushed her head and hands out of the box at the same time that the second assistant – hidden in the platform –

pushed her feet out of the other end. Goldin sawed through the box and could separate the two halves quite a long way. In fact, he could take the half with the assistant's head poking out of it as far away as he wanted.

In actual fact, Selbit's was by far the better trick. The size of Goldin's box made it easy for people to work out how he did it. But, when it came to publicity, Selbit was only half the man Goldin was. Before each of his shows, Goldin would arrange for an ambulance complete with doctors and nurses to drive through town announcing,

WE ARE GOING TO HORACE GOLDIN'S SHOW IN CASE THE SAW SLIPS!

He also placed adverts like this one in newspapers:

WANTED!

GIRLS TO BE SAWN IN HALF

Guarantee $10,000 in case of fatality.

Apply to: **HORACE GOLDIN, ROYAL ILLUSIONIST.**

The trick made Goldin very successful, so when Selbit decided to go to America later in 1921, there was bound to be trouble...

Dirty tricks

It's probably true to say that no one really expected Selbit and Goldin to become the best of friends, but any chance of them making even polite conversation with each other quickly disappeared once Selbit arrived in America. Goldin's management company promptly arranged for Goldin to perform in every town that Selbit was going to, one week before Selbit was due to be there. Selbit carried on with his tour anyway and eventually returned to England in 1922 to perform his saw trick in front of King George V at the Royal Variety Performance.

Before too long, Horace Goldin realized that his version of the trick needed improving, so he set about working on a new method. The finished product appeared in 1931 and was called "The Living Miracle". This time, he didn't bother with a box at all. His assistant simply lay on a table top and was sliced in half by a huge 90-centimetre (36 inch) circular saw. He even stopped the saw and turned the table sideways, so that the audience could see the girl sliced in two. Of course, a few seconds later she was miraculously back in one piece again and the audience went bananas.

For your amazement
In 1956, an Indian magician called Sorcar performed a trick on television that was similar to Goldin's "Living Miracle". He would chop his assistant, Dipty Dey, in half using a circular

*buzz saw. All was going swimmingly well until
the television show ran out of time and had to
finish before the audience had seen the two
halves of Dipty Dey put back together again. This
caused outrage and panic and thousands of
people rang the TV station concerned about her
condition. Of course, she was absolutely fine but
it wasn't until Dipty Dey was shown in one piece
on television again that the chaos died down.*

Three times a lady

In 1965, a magician called Robert Harbin took the
saw trick one step further. His version involved an
assistant standing in a box and being chopped into
three bits by two metal blades. The middle section –
containing the assistant's tummy – was then
pulled to one side leaving a gaping hole right
through her. What's more, all the time her head,
hand, foot and even tummy could be seen and
touched by members of the audience. Harbin called
her the Zig Zag Girl.

The Zig Zag girl was a massive success, so much
so that loads of other magicians started performing
the same trick. This made Robert Harbin very
angry and so in 1970 he released a book called *The
Magic of Robert Harbin,* which revealed the secret
of the trick.

"Great," you're probably thinking, "now we can
find out how it's done."

Well, not so fast... You see, the number of copies of
the book was strictly limited, the price was very
high and each person who bought a copy had to sign
an agreement not to tell anyone else the secret.

The death saw

The sawing-a-person-in-half illusion has been brought right up to date by modern magician David Copperfield. In fact, he doesn't even bother using a saw at all in one of his tricks, chopping his assistant into three pieces with a laser beam instead. Then he removes the middle piece altogether. Another of his illusions was recently voted the greatest magic trick in the world. It is called the "Death Saw". David Copperfield is tied down underneath a huge circular saw that is spinning very fast and getting closer and closer to him. He tries to escape but fails, and, in front of everyone's eyes, the saw appears to cut straight through him. His assistants then separate the two halves of his body and bring his head round so that he can see his feet.

Then the assistants put both halves back on either side of the saw, remove the saw and, hey presto, David's back in one piece again. It's an amazing effect, but sadly he hasn't written a book explaining how he does it.

Anyway, now for the bit you've all been waiting for...

Chopping your teacher in half

Oops sorry, Miraculo, we've run out of time for this one and have to get on.

But don't worry, maybe you can think of a way to do it yourself. (Only joking, of course!)

EXTREME ESCAPOLOGY

Good. Now that's out of the way, it's time for us to meet some of the bravest (or craziest) performers on Earth who, for some reason, thought that breaking free from handcuffs, ropes and suchlike would be an amazing spectacle. Here's a timeline of early escapology to get us started:

1600s

Chinese beggars perform on the streets for money. One of their amazing escape feats involves getting various parts of their bodies out of sealed wooden blocks.

Early 1700s

French entertainer La Trude begins to make escapes from prisoners' handcuffs. He is naturally very popular with prisoners, and is offered countless shows in jail.

1780s

The Italian performer Pinetti (yes, him again) includes escape acts in his show, using handcuffs and lengths of rope. He gains such a good reputation for escapology that he is invited to perform in front of King George III at Windsor castle in 1784.

Early 1800s

Stories begin to come out of India about magicians who can untie themselves from even the most complex of rope knots.

1870s

An Englishman by the name of Dr Redmond becomes very well known as a rope expert and handcuff manipulator. His patients are fascinated by his skills, but waiting times in his surgery are terrible.

Late 1800s

Native American Cree Indians are performing their own special version of the escape act. They tie up the arms and legs of a medicine man and place him inside the skin of an elk. He then has to figure out a way of breaking out.

Harry Houdini – the master arrives

All of these escapologists had been pretty impressive in their own ways, but a new figure was to burst on to the scene – someone who would tie them *all* up in knots. His name was Harry Houdini, and he changed the face of escapology for ever.

Houdini was born in Hungary in 1874 and named Ehrich Weiss. His family were very poor and, when Ehrich was four, they moved to America in search of a better life. His parents called him "Ehrie" as a nickname and, over time, he changed this to Harry. The Houdini part came from his favourite magician, a certain Mr Robert-Houdin (remember him – see page 110). Harry added an "i" to his hero's surname and suddenly the greatest magical name of all time had been created.

Harry was not your average child – at the age of eight he was already holding down several jobs. When he was 12, he ran away from home to travel round America.

Houdini started off as a double act with his brother, performing at beer halls and amusement parks. They called themselves "The Houdini Brothers", but after a while, Harry decided to go it alone. His act included lots of card and coin tricks. But, before long, Harry became fascinated by the art of escaping and started doing a handcuff escape as part of his show.

Houdini became so confident of his abilities that he started to issue challenges to the general public.

He would visit an area and plaster his posters where likely challengers might see them. The posters might have looked a bit like this...

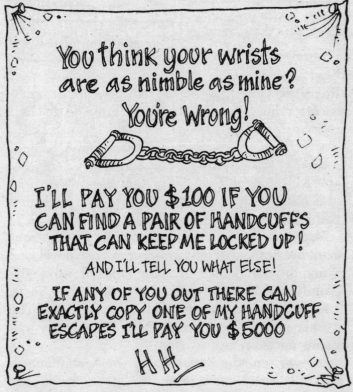

You think your wrists are as nimble as mine? You're Wrong!

I'LL PAY YOU $100 IF YOU CAN FIND A PAIR OF HANDCUFFS THAT CAN KEEP ME LOCKED UP!

AND I'LL TELL YOU WHAT ELSE!

IF ANY OF YOU OUT THERE CAN EXACTLY COPY ONE OF MY HANDCUFF ESCAPES I'LL PAY YOU $5000

HH

Loads of people took Houdini up on his challenges, trying a wide range of handcuffs on him. But no one could produce a pair that he couldn't escape from.

Houdini started to travel round America and Europe performing his act. On a trip to London in 1900, he demanded to be taken to police headquarters at Scotland Yard, and to be locked up in their most secure pair of handcuffs. The conversation between Harry and an English policeman went something like this:

Handcuffs were all well and good for Houdini, but soon he branched out into ropes. He developed many different ways of tying himself up – the thumb tie, the clothesline tie and the North American Indian tie were just a few of them. The crowds paid to see him and, to Houdini, it was money for old rope.

Forever on the lookout for new challenges, Houdini would often turn up at a prison and demand to be locked up. One of the most famous of these trips was a visit to a jail in Washington DC in 1906. Houdini demanded to be locked up in a cell, claiming that he'd be able to break out. To the amazement of the prison staff, he reappeared some time later. He'd not only managed to escape, but he'd unlocked many of the other cells and moved other prisoners around to boot.

Houdini's audiences really thought he had superhuman powers, but like all great show-offs in the world of magic, he had a few tricks up his sleeve...

How did they do that?
Houdini's escapology rules

1. Always have a secret pocket in your clothing and keep a small sharp knife in it.

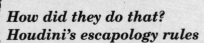

SECRET POCKET

2. It's vital to have a duplicate set of keys on your person.

3. Have an orchestra play really loud music while you're making loads of noise as you try to get out of a cabinet or cage.

4. *If you're being lowered into water whilst handcuffed and shackled inside a nailed box, make sure the box has a panel at one end that can be released.*

5. *When being locked up in several pairs of handcuffs, have the one with the most complicated lock put on last – highest up your arm. By the time you've got out of all the others, this one will slip easily over your wrists.*

The punch of death
Houdini loved publicity. To keep a high profile, he was forever inventing new ways to showcase his incredible range of talents. He even had a giant football made for one performance and invited a massive crowd to witness his escape. He once said,

'The public seek drama. Give them a hint of danger, perhaps of death and you will have them packing in to see you.'

Houdini lived a most extraordinary life and so it was fitting that he didn't die peacefully in his sleep. Backstage at a show in 1926, a student asked him if it was true that he could withstand punches to the stomach without getting hurt. Houdini said yes, but before he had time to clench his stomach muscles properly to protect himself, the student gave him an extremely hard punch. Even though he experienced great pain, he went on to perform the show. But Houdini had been injured very seriously and he died some time later.

Nearly an awful accident

Many performers have been inspired by Houdini and have copied some of his escapes or created new ones. They have met with varying degrees of success, although some have got themselves into a bit of bother:

● In 1996, US escapologist Robert Gallup performed the Death Dive. For this, he was tied up in chains and locked inside a steel cage. The cage was placed inside an aeroplane. When the plane was several thousand metres in the air, the cage was thrown out. Gallup had just 50 seconds to escape and pull on the parachute that was strapped to the outside of the cage. He made it just in time and seconds later the cage smashed on to the ground below.

So, do you think that escapology might be your bag? Well, our good friend Miraculo is standing by to show you, but before he sets things in motion, read and observe this next bit carefully.

AN EVEN MORE SERIOUS WARNING THAN THE FIRST ONE:

ALWAYS HAVE AN ADULT PRESENT WHEN YOU ATTEMPT THIS ESCAPE.

For this spectacular spectacle, you'll need a large bag, a long length of rope, a sheet, an assistant and, of course, an adult. DO NOT use a plastic bag. The best type of bag to use is a fabric one — you can make one out of a sheet. Clumsini — a bag, please!

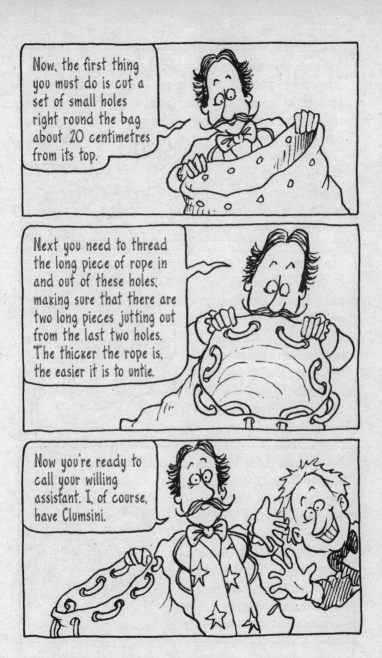

Now, the first thing you must do is cut a set of small holes right round the bag about 20 centimetres from its top.

Next you need to thread the long piece of rope in and out of these holes, making sure that there are two long pieces jutting out from the last two holes. The thicker the rope is, the easier it is to untie.

Now you're ready to call your willing assistant. I, of course, have Clumsini.

Ask your assistant to take hold of the two ends of jutting-out rope. Tell your audience that you're about to climb into the sack and be tied-up but will perform a dramatic escape.

Climb into the sack and, as you start to crouch down, pull a loop of rope towards you (with both hands) of at least 30 centimetres length. Your assistant will be loosely holding the two rope ends, so that you have enough slack to pull this loop towards you.

You are now inside the bag holding the loop. Your assistant ties up the two ends of rope in full view of the audience. Make sure they tie a simple knot or knots. An audience member can be invited onstage to check that the knot is secure.

The assistant then covers the whole sack with the sheet and the audience look on in wonder, thinking that there is no way you can escape from the sack. Yell, from inside the sack, the magic word – Escaponzo!

As soon as the sheet goes over the top of the sack, let go of the loop you're holding and you'll have enough room to get your hands out of the top of the sack. Untie the knot or knots as quickly as you can. As soon as you've done this, burst out of the sack, throw the sheet off and your audience will clap like thunder. You're an escapology star!

Thank you, Miraculo.

Now it's time to test your personal entertainment value in your very own...

PRIZE PERFORMANCE

From the smallest magic show in your bedroom to the most dazzling presentation in a huge theatre or on TV, if you want to be a magician, you must know your tricks inside out, back to front and upside down. Audiences want to be thrilled, amazed and excited – and part of the experience is the possibility that they might catch the magician out. If the magician isn't fully prepared, the audience may just do that.

If you want to be a success, you've got to work at it. You'll probably know yourself when you're good and ready, but to test yourself, show a trick to one or two people. If they beg you to do it again or to reveal how you did it, you're ready. If they sit there asking "What's magic about *that*?" you've probably got some more work to do.

So, without further ado, here's some advice:

Your props
● Try to make some props out of everyday objects. Audiences are often amazed by a trick done with something familiar.

I WILL NOW MAKE TEDDY DISAPPEAR...

- Use your imagination. If one of your tricks involves a ball, why not use an apple instead? Then, when you've finished, you can take a bite out of it or give it to someone in the audience as a finishing touch.

- Don't have too many props or your performing area might look messy. If you can use one prop again, then do so. You may want to decorate your stage with lots of pretty things, but that can make it difficult to move around and the audience will look at everything expectantly. They may be disappointed if something onstage is not used for a magic trick.

- Some props have secret pockets or special attachments so you may need to buy them from magic shops. Be warned though. Some magic equipment is very expensive. It may be worth phoning a shop before you visit to discover the cost of the particular item you're after. There are three types of secret pockets you should know about:

   a) The bag holder pocket – this opens at the bottom and lets the prop fall out into your hands.

   b) The dip pocket – this is a very small pocket on the outside of your costume that is placed at

arm's length, the place where your hands naturally hang when your arms are by your sides.
c) The toppit – an extra pocket inside a jacket or tail coat.

● Make sure both your clothes and props are appropriate for your image. Colourful and wacky clothes would suggest a funny, lively magician, whilst more traditional clothes, such as a top hat and dinner jacket would suggest a more serious magician.

● Consider what you need and when you need it. It's no good putting a particular prop in the back left-hand corner of the stage if, when you need it, you're in the front right-hand corner. Unless you have super-stretchy elastic arms of course...

● Whatever space you choose to perform in, make sure you know every nook, cranny, corner and crevice. Treat it like a second home, because the better you know your space, the more comfortable you'll feel performing in it.

Your patter
● It's not what you say, it's how and when you say it that is so important. Your magician's "patter" can also build up suspense for a trick. For example...

Do say:
"What you are about to witness is an extremely rare sight. It will baffle and bamboozle you and no matter how hard you try to work it out, you will be trying in vain. Only skilled masters in the ancient craft of magic are able to comprehend this awesome feat."

Don't say:
"Here's a trick that you might like. It's all right, but nothing special. You've all seen it a thousand times before. Anyone can do it and at the end you'll probably think, 'Oh, right, not bad.'"

● If you want to use a lot of comedy in your act, you'll need to learn a lot of jokes. But be warned ... it's very hard to tell a joke well, so you'll have to rehearse an awful lot and work on the timing. Short jokes, known as one-liners, might be best to start with.

● If you're a more serious magician, you may want to build a story around a trick or, if there is one, you could tell the real story about the trick.
● It's also a really good idea to have some patter prepared in case anyone in the audience tries to

heckle you or spoil your tricks. In most magical audiences, there is usually at least one "spoiler". Here's one way of dealing with them:

At the start of the act, give someone an envelope containing a piece of paper. Later, when the spoiler shouts out, "Oy, that wasn't much of a trick, that was rubbish!" you say, "I'm sorry you didn't like the trick. Maybe you'll prefer this one? It's a prediction I made earlier." You then ask the person holding the envelope to open it and read what's written on the paper, which is, "Prediction – at some point in the show someone will try to ruin it for everyone else. This person will be a horrible, nasty person and the rest of the audience will start to boo them."

● Don't spoil the surprise before the end of a trick by saying something like, "And when I open my hand I will have two red balls in it."

● Don't say what everyone can see that you're doing, for example, "I am now opening this box."

● Make your patter sound natural – even though you may have said it a thousand times before, it will be the first time your audience has heard it, so work at keeping your patter fresh.

- Don't make people suspicious – don't say, "I am going to cover the ball with this perfectly normal handkerchief which has not been changed in any way." The audience might not think the handkerchief is any different anyway, so don't put the idea into their heads.

Your audience

- Think about the position of the audience. Right in front of the stage is best. If they start sitting around the side, they may see how some of the tricks are done.
- When moving about the stage, walk behind things that you want to be seen – a prop or your assistant – and walk in front of them if what you are saying is more important.
- Don't turn your back on people – if the audience can't see your face, they could get bored. To move backwards, cross the stage diagonally, making sure that you have positioned the props and scenery so that you don't bump into them.
- A volunteer can be used to misdirect the audience. If you ask them to shuffle a pack of cards, the audience will look at the volunteer and not at you.

Your performance style

- Once you've got all the bits and pieces of your act sorted, you need to think about how they all fit together to make a whole show. It's not just a case of stringing a whole load of tricks together. There's no point in doing a trick that involves a complicated piece of gadgetry, which you'll have to get off the stage, followed by a trick that involves getting a different piece of gadgetry on to the stage. There should be a smooth flow between your tricks, so they blend into one another, almost as if the whole show is one long trick.

- Your first and last trick are very important. It's good to go out with a bang, but it's also good to come on to a bang. You want the audience to be impressed straight away, so make your first trick a really good 'un.

THANK YOU AND GOODNIGHT!

NOW THAT'S WHAT I CALL GOING OUT WITH A BANG!

- Professional magicians will have a producer who can watch them in rehearsal and point out things that they may not have noticed. You might be able to get a friend to watch you rehearse and give you their thoughts about your act.

- Don't mix styles – it will be odd for the audience if you start off as a funny magician and then suddenly change and become a mysterious one.

- Never repeat the same trick twice – the audience may beg you to do a trick again, but don't. Nothing is ever as good the second time around and there'll be no surprise, as the audience will know what is going to happen. It's also possible that they'll be able to work out how you did the trick if you repeat it.

- The old saying *practise makes perfect* could never be truer than for the magician. If you're serious about becoming a first-rate performer, you can never practise enough. In this book, you'll have learnt a handful of tricks, but there are thousands of others out there to be mastered, in books, magazines and on the web. The truly mystical magician never stops searching for new ways of presenting their act.

- If you can get hold of a video camera, film your act. Then you can play it back and watch yourself.

- Try to practise in front of a full-length mirror. That way, you'll see yourself as the audience sees you.

- Practise, practise, practise and practise some more. Practise in front of a mirror. Practise in front of next door's dog. Practise in front of next door's dog's mirror. Practise in front of anyone who'll watch you.

- Join a magic society. You need to be 18 to join the Magic Circle (details can be found on page 157), but you can join the Young Magic Circle if you're between the ages of 10 and 18. The YMC organizes an annual competition called the Young Magician of the Year. To enter, you do have to be a member of the YMC, so drop them a line and ask for an application form. But be warned – the quality of the acts in this competition is very high.

And finally...

You're almost ready to make that leap on to the magician's stage but, before you do, there's one last lesson – learn from the best. Go and watch as many magicians as you can. Study their techniques. Listen to what they say. Think about their tricks. If you can, go backstage and talk to them. Look at how they're dressed. You can pick up millions of little tips from other magicians and who better to start learning from than the Great Miraculo himself.

The half-whole rope

To perform my final trick, you must wear a watch. You'll also need a handkerchief (make sure it's clean) some scissors and two lengths of thin rope. One piece of rope should be about 15 cm long and the other about 40 cm. Clumsini – my props, please!

Before you perform this trick, take the shorter length of rope and make it into a loop. This will be your "secret" loop. When you've done this, stick it together at the non-loop end with a piece of clear adhesive tape, like so.

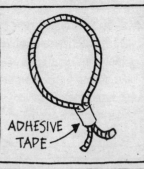

ADHESIVE TAPE

Tuck this secret loop under your watch. We'll call your watch hand, your "magic hand" and your other hand, "hand two".

MAGIC HAND

HAND TWO

You are now ready for the performance. Explain to the audience that you are about to cut a length of rope in half and then restore it to its full length. Take the longer length of rope with hand two and place it into the magic hand. The outer part of the magic hand must be facing the audience.

MAGIC HAND

Pull up the longer rope with hand two and make a loop that you hold in your magic hand. Now use hand two to cover this rope with the handkerchief.

When this is done, underneath the handkerchief, use hand two to quickly pull out the secret loop from your watch strap and pull it to the top of the magic hand. Then push down the longer loop into the palm of your hand so the audience won't be able to see it. Say the magic word – Halfwholeymoley!

HANDKERCHIEF

SECRET LOOP

FULL LENGTH ROPE

Pull off the handkerchief to reveal the secret loop (the audience of course thinks it's the loop of the longer piece) and ask a spectator to pick up the scissors and cut through the loop.

Place the handkerchief back over your magic hand and say the magic word again – Halfwholeymoley! Dramatically remove the handkerchief, taking the cut loop with it. Then reveal the longer length that is miraculously still in one piece! Take a bow as the sound of applause fills the air.

Hopefully, by now you'll have mastered enough tricks to start putting together a prize performance. So long as you practise your tricks, prepare your props and perfect your patter, nothing can stop you!

EPILOGUE

As if by magic, you've made it to the end of the book. It wasn't that tricky, was it? You've met some of the world's most magnificent magicians on your travels and discovered a gallery of triumphant tricks.

But if you think magic is exciting now, just think what it's going to be like in the future. David Copperfield already uses lasers in his show and Max Maven is experimenting with holograms and interactive magic. With technology changing and advancing at such a great pace, thousands of new, baffling and bemusing tricks and gadgets are just waiting to be invented. And, who knows, it could be you that creates one of them.

Today the demand for, and interest in, magic is bigger than ever. Even though we can travel faster than the speed of sound, talk to someone on the other side of the world as if they're next door and download billions of nuggets of information from the Internet in a matter of seconds, people are still amazed and blown away by even the simplest of tricks. The modern magician doesn't strut their stuff in a little booth on the village green – and some of the lucky ones are watched by millions on television, earn huge amounts of money, make best-selling videos and have hundreds of websites dedicated to them. Let's face it, magicians in the 21st century are massive stars.

And these magicians are continuing to perform more and more ambitious feats. In fact, you can bet your dinner money that as soon as the first theatre is built on the moon, a magician will be performing there.

So are you ready for that big move on to the magic stage? Have you performed your first show in front of an audience yet? Do you have what it takes to be a mystical marvel? What are you waiting for? Get your act together and start practising your bag of tricks. Remember, every great magician has to start somewhere.

Just think, you might come up with a magic trick that makes your school disappear.

Now that *would* be magic...

If you fancy finding out more about magic, these handy websites should help:

MAGIC SOCIETIES

- **The Magic Circle**
www.themagiccircle.co.uk
- **The Society of American Magicians**
www.magicsam.com
- **International Brotherhood of Magicians**
www.magician.org
- **www.theyoungmagiciansclub.co.uk**

A TINY SELECTION OF GOOD MAGIC WEBSITES (There are literally thousands of them out there.)

http://www.magicweek.co.uk
http://www.allmagicfinder.com
http://www.allmagicreviews.com
http://www.magicmagazine.com
http://www.davidblaine.com
http://www.lanceburton.com
http://www.davidcopperfield.com